IN ASSOCIATION WITH
IMPERIAL WAR MUSEUMS

BRITAIN AT WAR

FROM THE INVASION OF POLAND TO THE SURRENDER OF JAPAN

1939–1945

RICHARD OVERY

CARLTON
BOOKS

CONTENTS

THIS IS A CARLTON BOOK

This edition published in 2014 by Carlton Books Limited.
A division of the Carlton Publishing Group
20 Mortimer Street
London W1T 3JW

Printed in Dubai

A CIP catalogue for this book is available from the British Library

ISBN: 978 1 78097 526 9

REMOVABLE MEMORABILIA: Imperial War Museums: Items 1, 2 and 3; The National Archives, Kew: Items 4 and 5

INTRODUCTION

Britain fought the Second World War for longer than any of the other major powers between 1939 and 1945. The war against Germany began on 3 September 1939 and ended on 7 May 1945, when Britain still had four more months of war against the Japanese Empire. Britain also fought a truly global war. Across the major oceans, in the necklace of bases and colonies spread around the world, in the Indian sub-continent, across North Africa and the Middle East, even on the arduous Arctic supply routes to the Soviet Union, British sailors, airmen and soldiers were engaged in combat. British society at home had to cope with almost six years of blackout, food rationing, the threat of bombing, shortages of consumer goods and heavy taxes. It is small wonder that the war has remained a central part of British identity or that the historical memory of the war is still so alive more than 65 years after it ended.

There can be no masking the fact that for much of the first half of the war British forces faced a catalogue of defeats – Norway, Dunkirk, Greece, Crete, Malaya, Singapore, North Africa. Many of the earliest victories were against weak Italian or Vichy French opposition, in Madagascar, Ethiopia, Syria and Libya. But Britain's one advantage was the difficulty any major enemy faced in trying to defeat an island nation, surrounded by a powerful navy and a well-organized and up-to-date air force, and supported powerfully by the Commonwealth. The Battle of Britain was evidence for that, but so too was the resilience of British society during the Blitz. If Britain could not defeat the Axis single-handed, Germany and Italy could not, in nine months of trying, destroy British resistance in the home islands or in the Mediterranean.

The only way Britain could defeat the Axis, as Churchill and most of his public realised, was to persuade the United States to enter the conflict. Though sympathetic, Roosevelt found it difficult to persuade a cautious American public to accept that this was their war too. For over two years Britain and the Commonwealth carried the burden of the war. Much was achieved in the war at sea against the German submarine and surface fleet; British war production, centred on a worldwide web of raw material and food supplies from the Empire and Commonwealth, grew rapidly. The help given by the United States in the Atlantic battle and through Lend Lease supplies has been shown to be much less in the years before American entry than had once been thought. When the Soviet Union was attacked in June 1941, and the Hawaiian base at Pearl Harbor in December that year, Britain was already a powerful adversary in its own right, with the economic, scientific and technical skills necessary to wage a modern total war. The subsequent rise of the Soviet and American super-powers has dwarfed the contribution of the British Empire and Commonwealth and created an often distorted view of the reasons for victory.

This book is designed to show just what Britain did in the war, from early defeats to memorable victories. The ultimate success against the Axis states depended on the forging of the powerful Grand Alliance with the Soviet Union and the United States, but Britain's story in India, North Africa, the Italian campaign and the RAF bomber offensive against Germany and Italy, is a story in which the British military effort was an important, sometimes *the* most important element. The story is ably illustrated not only by the rich fund of photographs and images, but by the selection of key documents, some of grand policy, some the diaries and letters of ordinary servicemen. These documents give a flavour of the experience of war. They open a window onto an age that, though not forgotten, has become real history. They invite you, the reader, to share that history.

RICHARD OVERY

28 SEPTEMBER 1938–15 MARCH 1939

THE MUNICH CRISIS AND THE BREAK-UP OF CZECHOSLOVAKIA

After Hitler had taken over his Austrian homeland in March 1938, he began to make preparations to seize Czechoslovakia on the pretence that he was helping fellow Germans oppressed by Czech rule in the Sudeten areas of northern Czechoslovakia.

On 28 May, following the "Weekend Crisis" of 20/21 May, when the Czech government, fearing an imminent German invasion, ordered the mobilization of its forces, Hitler told his military commanders to plan a short, sharp war against the Czechs for the autumn of 1938. "I am utterly determined," he said, "that Czechoslovakia should disappear from the map."

Hitler thought he could isolate the Czechs and reach a quick military solution before the other powers intervened. The military planning went ahead, reflecting

Hitler's anxiety to wage a small, victorious war. In February, he had scrapped the War Ministry and taken over supreme command of the armed forces himself. The fight against the Czechs was a way of making his mark as a military leader, and an opportunity to improve Germany's economic and strategic position in central Europe.

The crisis could not be isolated: as pressure built up on the Czech government to make concessions to the Sudeten German minority, Britain and France both acted to try to find a negotiated political solution. France had treaty obligations to help the Czech state, and the Soviet Union was also committed to intervening, as long as France did so too. In neither state was there much enthusiasm for the prospect of war. Britain, meanwhile, had no treaty obligations, but the Prime Minister, Neville Chamberlain, hoped to use his influence to bring about a negotiated settlement as part of his strategy of "appeasement" of Germany. In August 1938, the British politician Lord Runciman was sent on a League of Nations mission to the Sudetenland and returned arguing that major concessions should be made by the Czech government to the German community.

Hitler stuck to his guns. German leaders attacked the Czechs in the press and on the platform. By the beginning of September, it seemed likely that Hitler would launch the military campaign in the near future. To avert this, on 15 September Chamberlain took the dramatic step of flying to meet Hitler at his mountain retreat at Berchtesgaden. Chamberlain conceded the need for self-determination, while Hitler promised not to make war on the Czechs, but he had no intention of honouring his word. Chamberlain flew again to meet the German leader on 22 September at Bad Godesberg, and this time the atmosphere was quite different, with Hitler insisting that he would occupy the Sudeten areas no later than 1 October. Chamberlain returned home to a cabinet now determined not to concede. France and Britain both prepared for war and on 26 September, Chamberlain sent his personal envoy, Sir Horace Wilson, to see Hitler and on the following day he made it absolutely clear that German violation of Czech sovereignty would mean war.

ABOVE: Commemorative medallion struck to mark Chamberlain's success at the Munich Conference in 1938.

OPPOSITE: Neville Chamberlain marches past an SS guard of honour at Oberwiesenfeld airport on his way to the Munich Conference on 29 September 1938, surrounded by National Socialist Party leaders.

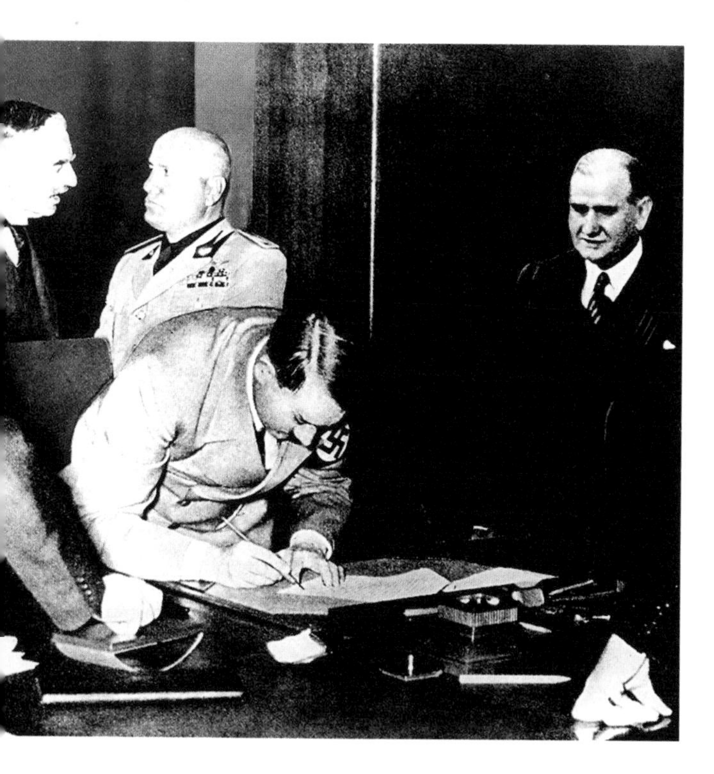

On 28 September, Hitler, with great reluctance, gave in. Under pressure from his party leaders and aware that German public opinion was strongly against a European war, he accepted Mussolini's suggestion of a summit conference in Munich, to which the Soviet Union was not invited. Hitler was sulky and ill at ease throughout the Munich discussions, which ended on 30 September with an agreement for the cession of the Sudeten areas to Germany and a timetable for German occupation. Unlike Japan in Manchuria and Italy in Abyssinia, Hitler's plan for a short war of conquest was frustrated. Munich is usually seen as a humiliating defeat for the British and French, but in reality it was a defeat for Hitler's plan for war. His frustration was to make it impossible to negotiate away the next crisis in 1939 over the City of Danzig.

Almost as soon as the ink was dry on the Munich Agreement, Hitler told his foreign minister, Joachim von Ribbentrop that he would march on Prague and smash the "Czech remnants" when the opportunity came. The Czech state was put under pressure to reach advantageous trade agreements to help German rearmament, and to concede the right to build a motorway across Czech land. In the Slovak areas, the Germans collaborated with the Slovak separatist movement, putting pressure on the Prague government to grant independence. Bit by bit, the Czech lands were being drawn into the German orbit.

We, the German Führer and Chancellor and the British Prime Minister, have had a further meeting today and are agreed in recognising that the question of Anglo-German relations is of the first importance for the two countries and for Europe.

We regard the agreement signed last night and the Anglo-German Naval Agreement as symbolic of the desire of our two peoples never to go to war with one another again.

We are resolved that the method of consultation shall be the method adopted to deal with any other questions that may concern our two countries, and we are determined to continue our efforts to remove possible sources of difference and thus to contribute to assure the peace of Europe.

Neville Chamberlain

September 30, 1938

The isolation of Czechoslovakia after Munich also encouraged its other neighbours to join in the search for spoils. On 30 October, Poland demanded the cession of the Teschen region and the Czech government complied; on 2 November, territorial concessions were made to Hungary in southern Slovakia. Germany then demanded that the Prague government turn Czechoslovakia into a virtual German dependency. It was only a matter of time before the remaining Czechoslovak area was broken up. On 12 January 1939, orders were issued to German army units to prepare to occupy the Czech lands, though no final decision had yet been taken. The immediate trigger for the actual invasion was the breakdown in relations between the Czechs and the Slovaks: in March, the Slovak government in Bratislava refused to abandon its claim for independence, thereby provoking the Prague government to declare martial law and send troops into Slovakia. The leader of the Slovak separatists, Jozef Tiso, fled to Vienna and then to Berlin, where Hitler encouraged him to call the Slovak assembly together, which then declared independence on 14 March.

The Czech president, Emil Hácha, took the train to Berlin to seek Hitler's advice, and in the early hours of 15 March, after Hermann Göring had painted a vision for him of German bombers over Prague, he invited Germany to occupy and "protect" Czechoslovakia. At six o'clock in the morning, German forces occupied the Czech provinces of Bohemia and Moravia, while the Hungarian army seized control of some Slovak provinces. The following day, the Czech areas were declared a German protectorate and the former German foreign minister, Constantin von Neurath, was appointed first "Reich Protector". Major Czech businesses, including the famous Skoda armaments complex, were brought under direct German control, and Czech military supplies helped to equip 15 German infantry divisions and four armoured divisions for the coming conflict. Slovakia was made an independent pro-German state under Tiso and remained a close ally down to 1944.

The occupation of the rest of Czechoslovakia tore up the short-lived Munich agreement. The British and French governments could do nothing to save Czechoslovakia, which had not actually been invaded but forced to "invite" German occupation, but the decision to incorporate non-German peoples in the new German empire prompted Neville Chamberlain on 17 March to make a powerful speech condemning German action. The Prague occupation had finally convinced him that there was no room for a negotiated settlement and he warned that if any nation tried to dominate Europe, Britain would resist "to the utmost of its power". A few days later, prompted by warnings from the security services of an imminent German occupation of Poland, Chamberlain offered the historic guarantee of Polish sovereignty in the House of Commons on 31 March. The Czech crisis had paved the way for the final countdown to war.

OPPOSITE, TOP: Adolf Hitler signing the Munich Agreement in the early hours of 30 September 1938 after a dozen hours of negotiation. Behind him are Chamberlain and Mussolini, to his left Daladier.

OPPOSITE, BELOW: German troops march into Prague during the occupation on 15 March 1939. Following the takeover the Czech army was disbanded.

ABOVE: Chamberlain's "pjece of paper", the Anglo-German declaration of 30 September 1939 signed by Hitler and Chamberlain.

RIGHT: Enthusiastic Germans remove the frontier posts separating Germany from Czechoslovakia. The Czech lands became a Reich Protectorate, while Slovakia won its "independence".

1–3 SEPTEMBER 1939

WAR IS DECLARED

The German invasion of Poland on 1 September 1939 was the culmination of a plan codenamed "Case White" which had first been drawn up by the German armed forces on Hitler's orders in April.

The war against Poland was not a conflict Hitler had initially expected. After Munich, he assumed that the Poles would be drawn into the German sphere of influence. He wanted them to readjust the status of Danzig, a city supervized by the League of Nations to allow Poland access to the sea, to become a German city as it had been before 1919, and to hand back the rich industrial areas of Silesia, which had been given to Poland after a plebiscite in 1919.

The Poles refused any concessions and Hitler, frustrated at not getting his small war in 1938 against the Czechs, decided to punish the Poles by seizing the areas by force. He argued to the doubters in Berlin that Britain and France would protest but would not intervene. After signing the pact with the Soviet Union, Hitler was certain that the risk was much reduced. A pretence at last-minute negotiation in the final days of August was designed to make it seem as if Germany had a legitimate cause for war, though in fact the SS – the elite National Socialist security force – planned to stage a frontier incident to make it look as if the Poles were the aggressors. An attack by Germans wearing Polish uniforms on the frontier station at Gleiwitz on the night of 31 August/1 September was the signal. The order went out for the 1.5-million-strong German army, supported by more than 1,500 aircraft, to move forward in the first test of what came to be known as blitzkrieg or lightning war.

he German plan was for a two-pronged assault from East Prussia in the north and German Silesia in the south

aimed towards the Polish capital, Warsaw. In the vanguard were five Panzer divisions of fast-moving mobile troops grouped around 300 tanks, supported by dive-bombers and fighters. It was the first time this new form of swift battlefield attack, using modern weaponry, had been tried out. The Polish army, almost one million strong, resisted bravely, but was overwhelmed by the Germans' striking power. The small Polish air force of around 400 planes was eliminated, though the German air force suffered 564 aircraft destroyed or damaged. Within a week of the start of the campaign German forces were 40–65km (25–40 miles) from Warsaw, tightening a noose around the encircled Polish armies. A final Polish stand was made at Warsaw and the fortress of Modlin to the north, but following the heavy bombing of the capital, Polish forces there surrendered on 27 September. Around 100,000 Polish soldiers escaped across neighbouring borders but 694,000 went into captivity. The German forces had lost some 13,000 men, the Poles 70,000: the first test of the rearmed German forces was a complete success.

The following day, 28 September, German and Soviet commanders met to decide the demarcation line between them. A new agreement was reached, the German–Soviet Treaty of Friendship, which sealed the partition of Poland, granting Warsaw to the area occupied by the Germans. Jews were victimized from the start and in November 1940 they were forced into a sealed ghetto in the city. Behind the German armies, Hitler had sent special "action squads" (Einsatzgruppen) manned by security agents and SS men, who began the systematic killing of all Polish intellectuals, nationalist politicians and government elite in a pattern that was to be repeated across Europe in the grim years of German occupation. By the end of the war, more than six million Poles, including three million Polish Jews, had been killed.

Der Oberste Befehlshaber der Wehrmacht — Berlin, den 39.
OKW/WFA Nr. 170 /39 g.K.Chefs. L I

8 Ausfertigungen
2. Ausfertigung.

Weisung Nr. 1
für die Kriegführung.

1.) Nachdem alle politischen Möglichkeiten erschöpft sind, um auf friedlichem Wege eine für Deutschland unerträgliche Lage an seiner Ostgrenze zu beseitigen, habe ich mich zur gewaltsamen Lösung entschlossen.

2.) Der Angriff gegen Polen ist nach den für Fall Weiss getroffenen Vorbereitungen zu führen mit den Abänderungen, die sich beim Heer durch den inzwischen fast vollendeten Aufmarsch ergeben.

Aufgabenverteilung und Operationsziel bleiben unverändert.

Angriffstag: 1.9.39.

Angriffszeit ....

Diese Zeit gilt auch für die Unternehmungen Gdingen - Danziger Bucht und Brücke Dirschau.

3.) Jm Westen kommt es darauf an, die Verantwortung für die Eröffnung von Feindseligkeiten eindeutig England und Frankreich zu überlassen. Geringfügigen Grenzverletzungen ist zunächst rein örtlich entgegen zu treten.

Die von uns Holland, Belgien, Luxemburg und der Schweiz zugesicherte Neutralität ist peinlich zu achten.

OPPOSITE: German tanks and armoured vehicles cross a bridge over a river as they advance into Poland on 6 September 1939.

ABOVE: Hitler's first War Directive issued on 21 August 1939 ordered the invasion of Poland.

BELOW: A Polish mounted brigade in 1939. Poland still used cavalry armed with lances and sabres, which were no match for modern German equipment.

At 11.15 on Sunday morning, 3 September 1939, the British Prime Minister announced over the radio from 10 Downing Street that Britain was once again at war with Germany.

No sooner had he finished speaking than the air-raid sirens set up in the capital let out their mournful wailing noise. All over southern England people dived for bunkers, cellars or doorways. Neville Chamberlain was reluctant to leave his office but was finally persuaded to go down into the shelter prepared for him. It turned out to be a false alarm, but the initial panic reflected the profound fear that the new war would be won or lost by bombing with gas, germ warfare and fire.

Britain's decision to go to war was almost inevitable once German forces had crossed the Polish frontier. As early as February, Chamberlain had pledged Britain to defend France, and from March the British and French military worked on a war plan so that they could make advance preparations. They expected to face a three-year war of attrition, a repeat of the First World War in which German resistance would be sapped by economic blockade, food shortages and, if necessary, by the bombing of German cities. In France, opinion rallied to the idea of confronting fascism, though right-wing groups stuck posters up on the walls of Paris asking "Who Will Die for Danzig?". By August, Britain and France were mobilizing, ration-books were already being distributed to local authorities and millions of children and mothers prepared for evacuation away from the threatened cities. The British public steeled itself for the coming conflict "like the glassy sea when a hurricane comes", wrote the journalist Malcolm Muggeridge. Intelligence sources confirmed that German armies were moving into position. Although the British and French governments promised to help the Poles when war came, they privately agreed that assistance was useless and made no plans to do so. They hoped to restore a free Poland when the war was over and planned to hold tight on the western front.

In the last days before war there was a sudden flurry of activity. A Swedish businessman and friend of Hermann Göring, Birger Dahlerus, was despatched to London to see if the British could be separated from France by negotiating a deal. His mission was a blind, intended to confuse

the British while Germany attacked Poland. At the last minute, after the German attack, Mussolini tried to intervene as he had at Munich, but the British and French governments, though willing to consider sensible proposals, were not prepared to allow Germany to occupy Poland. An ultimatum was delivered to Germany at 9 a.m. on 3 September by the British Ambassador, Sir Nevile Henderson, who found no one at the German Foreign Office except for Hitler's interpreter, Paul Schmidt, to whom he gave the solemn document. Schmidt hurried over to the Reich chancellery to read the ultimatum to a silent Hitler, who at the end turned to his Foreign Minister von Ribbentrop, and asked in harsh tones, "What now?" War could no longer be avoided. Chamberlain and the French premier, Edouard Daladier, would both have preferred peace, but could not abandon their commitment to Poland and to each other. The British ultimatum ran out at 11 a.m., the French later, at 5.00 p.m., and India, Australia and New Zealand declared war the same day. South Africa and Canada followed shortly after on 6 and 10 September respectively. In France, six million men were in the process of mobilization. The American Ambassador watched French troops leaving Paris: "The men left in silence. There were no bands, no songs," but only "self-control and a quiet courage".

OPPOSITE, TOP: A newspaper vendor in Paris carries news of the British declaration of war on Germany, 3 September 1939. The French ultimatum expired six hours later than the British at 5.00 p.m. on the same day.

OPPOSITE, BELOW: Londoners run for shelter minutes after the British declaration of war on 3 September when the first (false) air-raid alarm was sounded.

ABOVE: Evacuees leave British cities. In Britain, official programmes covered evacuation of 1.75 million, with two million more expected to arrange private evacuation.

MAP KEY

- final Polish pockets of resistance
- German-Soviet demarcation line, 30 September 1939

POLAND, SEPTEMBER 1939

Baltic Sea
Gdynia 14 Sep.
Königsberg
Danzig
EAST PRUSSIA
LITHUANIA
XXX I
XXX XIX GUDERIAN
XXXX 4 KLUGE
XXXXX NORTH BOCK
Allenstein
Marienwerder
XXXX 3 KUECHLER
XXX XXI
Grodno
GERMANY
Stettin
Chelmno
XXX II
XXXXX BELORUSSIAN
Slutsk
Berlin
Oder
Küstrin
Frankfurt
Warta
XXX III
Torun
Vistula
Lomza
Bialystok
POLAND
Poznan
XXXX POZNAN
XXXX POMORZE
Kutno
Warsaw
XXXX MODLIN
XXX XIX GUDERIAN
Pripet
Bzura River, 9–10 Sep.
surrenders 27 Sep.
Brest-Litovsk
Pinsk
Cottbus
Glogau
XXX X
Lodz
XXX XIX HOEPPNER
XXXX PRUSY
XXX XIII
XXXX LODZ
XXXX 8 BLASKOWITZ
Dresden
Breslau
XXX XI
XXX XIV
Radom
Bug
Marshes
Chelm
XXXX KRAKOW
XXXXX UKRAINIAN
Elbe
XXX IV
XXX XV
XXXX 10 REICHENAU
XXX VII
Gleiwitz
Katowice
XXX VIII
Vistula
Prague
Krakow
XXXX CARPATHIAN
PROTECTORATE OF BOHEMIA AND MORAVIA
XXXXX SOUTH RUNDSTEDT
XXX XVII
XXX XXII
Gorlice
Jaroslaw
Lwów
Tarnopol
Dniester
Brünn
XXXX 14 LIST
SLOVAKIA
XXX XVIII

13 DECEMBER 1939

THE BATTLE OF THE RIVER PLATE

On 26 September 1939, Adolf Hitler ordered two German "pocket" battleships, *Deutschland* and *Admiral Graf Spee*, to begin intercepting and destroying British merchant ships in the Atlantic Ocean.

The ships had been built in the early 1930s when Germany was still restricted to vessels of 10,000 tons. They were designed to maximize effective firepower despite the weight restriction and *Graf Spee* mounted six 280mm (11-inch) guns. The job of the pocket battleships was to destroy trade by what was called "merchant raiding", not to fight the Royal Navy, and the *Graf Spee's* captain, Hans Langsdorff, was under strict orders not to engage enemy warships. The German Navy High Command wanted no repeat of the disaster of the First World War, when a squadron under Admiral von Spee, whose name now adorned Langsdorff's ship, had been defeated off the Falkland Islands. Between September and

OPPOSITE: The German pocket battleship *Graf Spee* on fire after being scuttled in the estuary of the River Plate, 17 December 1939.

LEFT: Damage to the director tower of HMS *Achilles* after being hit by splinters from a 200-mm (11-inch) shell from the *Graf Spee* on 13 December 1939.

ABOVE: The cap worn by a German Naval Rating aboard the Admiral *Graf Spee*.

9 December, he sank or captured nine merchant ships but the wear and tear on the ship's less effective diesel-powered engines meant that a lengthy return trip to Germany became necessary for refitting. Before his departure Langsdorff decided to disobey his orders and find a weak British naval target to destroy. He sailed for Montevideo, where he was told a small British escort force would be leaving on 10 December. This would bring him a cheap victory and assure a triumphal homecoming to Germany.

Unknown to Langsdorff, British naval force "G" had been formed under Commodore Henry Harwood to hunt down the merchant raider. Even though one doomed merchant ship had managed to send out a signal with its position, tracking down the *Graf Spee* in an area as vast as the South Atlantic was extremely difficult, but on instinct Harwood decided on 9 December to make for the mouth of the River Plate. Early in the morning of 13 December, the German ship spotted the British force. Langsdorff ordered full steam ahead, and only too late discovered that he was engaging one heavy and two light cruisers rather than the small escort vessels he had expected. Though outgunned, Harwood decided at once to engage the *Graf Spee*. While the heavy cruiser *Exeter* moved west to draw the German fire, Harwood took the light cruisers *Ajax* and *Achilles* – the latter manned largely by New Zealanders – northeast to attack from the other side.

In a little over an hour of firing, *Exeter* was crippled and the two light cruisers badly damaged by the large 280mm (11-inch) shells from the German guns. But the determined British attack produced 20 hits on the *Graf Spee* which left her in no condition to pursue the enemy or even to finish off the *Exeter*. Reluctantly, Langsdorff broke away and made off for Montevideo in neutral Uruguay.

Anxious that a stronger Royal Navy force was approaching and pressed by the Uruguayan authorities to leave, Langsdorff realized that his position was hopeless. He ordered the crew to leave the ship, set charges and sailed the ship out to sea where, at 8.45 in the evening on 17 December 1939, it blew up, sinking at once. Langsdorff ensured that his crewmen were interned in Argentina, which was sympathetic to the Axis, then wrote a suicide note accepting full blame for the disaster. Laying out his battleship's ensign, he shot himself.

Harwood was the one who returned home to glory. He was knighted and made a Rear Admiral, while his commanders all won high decorations. Winston Churchill went to Plymouth to welcome the damaged *Exeter*, which was later sunk by the Japanese in 1942. The Battle of the River Plate was Britain's first wartime victory and one of the few pieces of action throughout the so-called Phoney War which stretched from September 1939 to April 1940, when Hitler invaded Denmark and Norway.

9 APRIL–9 JUNE 1940

THE INVASION OF NORWAY

During the early months of 1940, both sides eyed Scandinavia as a possible area for military action.

The Allies explored the possibility of cutting Germany off from her essential supplies of high-quality Swedish iron ore by mining Norwegian waters. The French government advocated the possible military occupation of the ore-producing areas. The German navy began to explore the idea of occupying Norway to protect the mineral resources and provide it with a springboard for attacks against Allied shipping in the North Atlantic. On 5 February 1940, Hitler ordered planning to begin for Operation "Weserübung", the possible occupation of Denmark and Norway.

The stakes were raised when Philip Vian, the captain of the British destroyer HMS *Cossack*, found the German tanker *Altmark* anchored in Norwegian waters. The German ship carried 299 British prisoners captured from ships sunk by the *Graf Spee*. To avoid offending the Norwegian government, Vian was ordered not to intervene, but he disobeyed orders, boarded the *Altmark* and rescued the British sailors. The exploit was well received by the British public, but it alerted Hitler to the real danger of British intervention, while Anglo–Norwegian relations reached a low ebb. In early April, Winston Churchill, as First Lord of the Admiralty, ordered the mining of Norwegian coastal waters, which began on 8 April, but Hitler had already decided on 2 April to launch a pre-emptive strike on his northern flank. Operation "Weserübung" began on the morning of 9 April, when two divisions of German troops entered Denmark almost unopposed. A large flotilla of ships made for the Norwegian capital, Oslo, and for the smaller

port cities on the long Norwegian coastline. They were supported by a specially organized 10th Flying Corps, whose job was to ferry paratroops to Norway and to prevent the Royal Navy from intervening.

The German campaign took the Allies by surprise and succeeded within days in seizing most of Norway, despite the loss of a large part of the surface fleet and numerous smaller vessels, including the newly launched heavy cruiser *Blücher*, which was sunk by Norwegian shore batteries as it approached Oslo, carrying onboard the German administrators and Gestapo officials destined to rule occupied Norway. The new fast battle cruisers *Scharnhorst* and *Gneisenau* were also damaged in combat with the Royal Navy. On 8 April, the cruiser *Hipper* was holed by the British destroyer HMS *Glowworm*, which rammed the much larger ship, blew up and sank. However, an Allied expeditionary force which landed at Narvik on 14 April and near Trondheim on 18 April was pinned down by German forces, and by 3 May was compelled to evacuate from the Trondheim area, despite the destruction of most of the covering German naval force. The battle around Narvik was hampered by continuous air attacks against British shipping, but by 8 June, with the Battle of France reaching its critical climax, Allied forces were evacuated, along with the Norwegian royal family and government, and with the Norwegian surrender two days later, German control of Norway was complete. King Haakon, however, insisted on maintaining a state of war from exile in London. German losses totalled 3,700 men, Allied forces the same number. The German navy lost a large part of the surface fleet, including three cruisers and 10 destroyers, and was never again in a position to mount a major operation. The Royal Navy lost an aircraft carrier, two cruisers and nine destroyers but remained a formidable force. Hitler secured the supply of Swedish iron ore and ordered Trondheim turned into a major German naval base. The remains of the vast concrete submarine pens can be seen to this day.

No figure so dominates the early history of the Second World War as Winston Leonard Spencer Churchill. He came to

ABOVE: Churchill stands outside the Admiralty building in London's Whitehall on 17 September 1939, two weeks after his appointment as First Lord of the Admiralty, the same post he held at the beginning of the First World War.

ABOVE, TOP: British forces near the town of Trondheim on the north Norwegian coast during the attempt in May 1940 to wrest control from the German occupiers.

OPPOSITE: German soldiers deploy heavy artillery against Allied forces in May 1940 around Narvik, which the Allies captured on May 28 but abandoned 11 days later.

symbolize British resistance to Hitler, and his determination to fight on, whatever the odds, made him into a legend in his own lifetime. He had always harboured the ambition to be a great war leader but during the 20 years since the end of the First World War, Churchill had experienced increasing political decline and isolation and his choice as Britain's wartime Prime Minister to succeed Neville Chamberlain came through luck as much as ambition. Only in office did the full scale of Churchill's leadership abilities finally emerge.

There were many reasons why Churchill's parliamentary colleagues were dubious about him. He was flamboyant, intemperate and unpredictable – a larger-than-life personality who had spent a political lifetime making enemies. He was first elected to Parliament in 1900 as a Conservative, switched to the Liberal Party in 1904 and then back to the Conservatives in 1924. Churchill had strong views on empire and hated communism. He expressed himself forcefully, and followed his own instincts as much as political common sense. He was regarded as an unsuccessful Chancellor of the Exchequer between 1924 and 1929, and in the 1930s found himself in the political wilderness. During this time he wrote extensively, predominantly autobiography and history, including his famous *Life of Marlborough*, and he campaigned on issues that were far from popular. He was opposed to making concessions to Gandhi's

ABOVE: British troops in northern Norway with a French Hotchkiss H39 light tank. The flow of military equipment was too slow to halt the German advance and after 10 May Allied priorities lay in France.

LEFT: Neville Chamberlain and his wife walk through St. James' Park in central London on 10 May 1940, the day of his resignation. Chamberlain remained a firm supporter of Churchill until his death in November.

OPPOSITE: Churchill gives the famous V for Victory sign to a crowd outside the Sheffield City Hall in November 1941. The sign was first used by English archers in the Middle Ages to taunt their French opponents who used to cut off the middle fingers of English prisoners to prevent them drawing a bow.

Indian nationalists and demanded that Britain rearm as fully as possible to meet the likely threat from Hitler. His reputation as a warmonger and reactionary were out of step with the mood of pacifism and appeasement which prevailed up to Munich and even beyond.

Churchill was a powerful political figure nonetheless, and in September 1939 Chamberlain invited him back into the cabinet as First Lord of the Admiralty. Although Churchill oversaw the disastrous Norwegian campaign, it was Chamberlain who took the blame when the war went wrong, and the public mood then swung strongly against Chamberlain's handling of the conflict, meaning a successor as Prime Minister was needed. Churchill was not the first choice of the Conservative majority in Parliament, but he was a figure that the opposition Labour Party and the trades unions would work with. On 9 May, one day before German armies attacked in the west, Churchill was called to Chamberlain's office together with the Foreign Secretary, Lord Halifax, whom Chamberlain would have preferred as his successor. Churchill recalled in his post-war account that he said little, waiting for Halifax to speak. Finally, the silence was broken when Halifax announced that he did not feel he could cope with being a war leader. Churchill was left unopposed; he wrote later that at that moment, "I felt as if I was walking with destiny, and that all my past life had been a preparation for this hour and for this trial…".

When Churchill arrived in the Commons on 13 May, there was no more than a ripple of applause, while the Lords greeted his appointment in silence. Within weeks, Churchill found himself the leader of a nation defeated in France and threatened with invasion. Although there were some British politicians who favoured a compromise with Hitler, from the day of his appointment Churchill never wavered in his determination to defeat Hitlerism and to rally British society to fight the war to the end. It is this defiance at a critical moment in the British war effort that moulded the Churchill legend. The public forgot his chequered past and rallied to his summons.

10–27 MAY 1940

GERMANY INVADES IN THE WEST

On 10 May 1940 German forces launched a series of swift operations against the Dutch, Belgian and French armed forces.

Hitler had wanted to invade in the West in November 1939 but bad weather prevented it. During the spring, German military planners prepared a campaign based on a rapid defeat of Allied forces by striking with armour and aircraft through the heavily wooded Ardennes sector of the front, where the French Maginot Line fortifications were weakest. The balance of forces between the two sides favoured the Western Allies in army divisions (144 to 141), artillery pieces (13,974 to 7,378) and tanks (3,384 to 2,445); German fighter and bomber forces were outnumbered on paper by the Allies (3,254 to 3,562), but both the French and British chose to keep large air forces away from the battlefield, defending the rest of France and mainland Britain.

The rapid German advance was based on a number of daring strategic strokes and the miscalculation of the Allies. The Western plan was based on a rapid movement of forces into Belgium and the Netherlands to counter the expected German attack. After German forces attacked the Netherlands and seized the key Belgian fortress of Eben Emael with the first successful airborne assault on 10 May, the Allies attempted to move forces into the Low Countries to halt the German advance. Dutch resistance crumbled and within a few days Belgian, British and French forces were in retreat. Unknown to the Western Allies, large German formations of armoured divisions, heavily protected by fighters, had by 12 May mustered in the Ardennes forest, considered virtually impassable by the French High Command, and stood poised for an historic breakthrough.

Under the command of General von Kleist, Guderian's Panzer divisions broke across the Meuse River on 13 May and, heavily supported by the Junkers Ju87 dive bomber and large numbers of medium bombers, unhinged the whole French front by driving a powerful wedge between two French armies, General Hutzinger's 2nd and General Corap's 9th. "There has been a rather serious hitch at Sedan," reported Colonel Lacaille, chief-of-staff of the 2nd

Army. The "hitch" turned into a rout. The French front collapsed and German commanders began the successful rush for the coast in the hope of encircling and destroying all the remaining Allied armies in the pocket. By 19 May Guderian's tanks had reached the Channel coast at Abbeville. A small number of counterattacks by French and British forces held up what was close to becoming a foregone conclusion. On 28 May, after a brave defence of western Belgium, the Belgian king surrendered. The Netherlands had capitulated on 14 May, following a fierce air bomb attack on the Dutch port of Rotterdam.

The rapid German advance created panic in the French leadership. British reinforcements were slow to arrive and the bulk of British air power remained in Britain to defend against a possible German air assault. On 16 May Winston Churchill flew to Paris where he was told that there was no French reserve left to hold up the German advance. The same day the French premier, Paul Reynaud, told the French parliament that only a miracle could save France from defeat. As the noose tightened around the trapped British and French forces in northern France, plans were made to try to hold the line of the River Somme, where more than 20 years before some of the bloodiest battles of the First World War had been fought. On 23 May the British military Chiefs-of-Staff decided that the war in France was lost and prepared to abandon their ally. On 27 May British forces began to evacuate from the northern French port of Dunkirk. France was forced to fight on alone.

ABOVE: Men of the Royal Fusiliers man a Bren gun position at the front near the Saint Francois-Lacroix, 3 January 1940. By May 1940 there were 394,165 members of the BEF on the French/Belgian border. 237,319 of these were employed in front line duties.

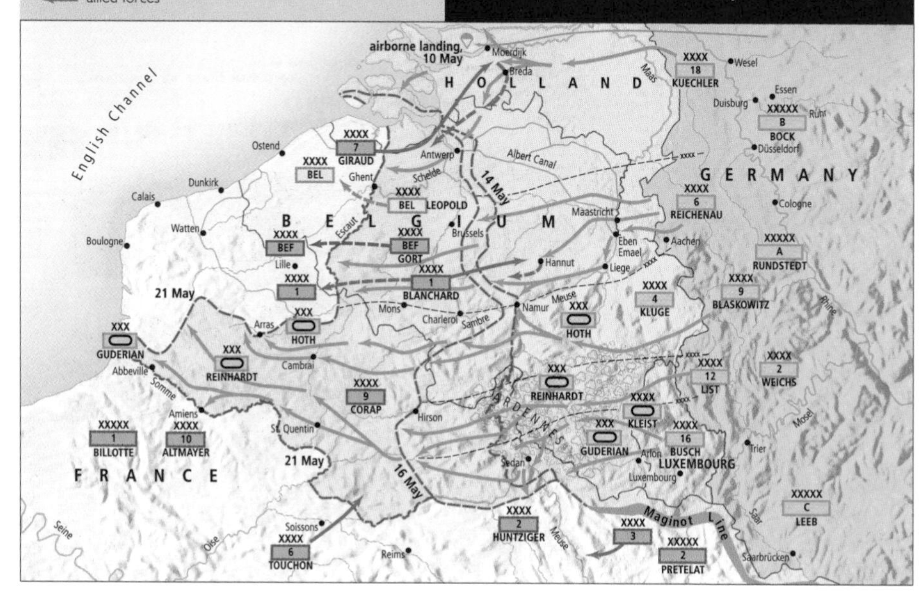

OPPOSITE: The Junkers Ju87B "Stuka" was the most famous of the German dive bombers and used to devastating effect during Germany's Blitzkreig of the West. However, as learned during the Battle of Britain, it required total air superiority to be effective because it was slow and cumbersome.

27 MAY–4 JUNE 1940
DUNKIRK

As German forces pressed forward into France they opened up a wide gap between the British Expeditionary Force in northern France and the bulk of the French army to the south.

By the fourth week of May, German thrusts had also separated the BEF from the crumbling Belgian army, which capitulated three days later. There existed a very real danger that the entire British force would be encircled and captured, but on 23 May von Runstedt halted the armoured forces, and the following day Hitler, uncertain about the strength of the French army to the south, concurred. The German armour stopped in front of a network of water-courses surrounding the area around Lille and Dunkirk now occupied by the BEF and a substantial number of trapped French divisions. This pause allowed a rough perimeter defence to be established by the Allies. On 26 May, the British government ordered Lord Gort, the BEF commander, to evacuate as many troops as he could from France. The evacuation was masterminded by Vice Admiral Bertram Ramsay, who later, as Naval Commander, organized the shipping for the D-Day invasion. Given the codename Operation "Dynamo" – after the small dynamo room in the Dover cliffs used as the operational base – the saving of the BEF became one of the great legends in Britain's war effort.

The fighting retreat begun around 21 May was among the fiercest action of the campaign. The troops holding the British line at Arras were ordered to "fight to the last

ABOVE: A British anti-aircraft gun abandoned at Dunkirk, June 1940. Most of the equipment of the British Expeditionary Force had to be left behind in France.

LEFT: Officers of the Royal Ulster Rifles awaiting evacuation at Bray Dunes, about 8km (5miles) from Dunkirk.

OPPOSITE BELOW: British forces line up on the beach at Dunkirk, waiting to be evacuated.

man and the last round". When German attacks resumed on 26 May, every mile of ground was contested. Under a hail of bombs from German aircraft, an estimated 850–950 small ships and larger naval and merchant vessels plied back and forth, carrying British troops between Dunkirk and the southern British ports. In addition to Royal Navy vessels and large steamers, there came lifeboats and trawlers. The Port of London Authority sent nine tugs drawing barges behind them. Fortunately, British fighter aircraft were able to reach Dunkirk from British bases and kept up regular sorties against German units, though 177 British aircraft were lost. When the weather was clear, German aircraft exacted a heavy toll: on 1 June, three destroyers were sunk and Ramsay ordered sailings only at night.

During the eight days of the evacuation, an estimated 338,000 troops were rescued including 110,000 French servicemen, most of whom were saved only on the last two days after Ramsay was ordered to send back the big ships to rescue non-British forces as well. A mixture of British and French units continued to defend the pocket, and for many of them, including the 51st Highland Division, forced to surrender in mid-June, evacuation was not possible. Some 8,000 British soldiers went into captivity. On the evacuation beaches discipline was hard to maintain and panicking soldiers were sometimes killed or beaten to keep order, while British forces also shot French soldiers suspected of spying or betrayal. On 27 May, a group of the Royal Norfolks was caught by the SS "Death's Head" Division, commanded by General Theodor Eicke, former commandant of Dachau, and 97 of them were murdered in cold blood.

The Dunkirk evacuation was both a victory and a defeat. It showed how important was British naval power and it also provided a taste of the conflict between the two air forces that later dominated the summer and autumn of 1940. German aircraft losses during the Battle of France were higher than in the later Battle of Britain. Yet Dunkirk did mean an ignominious end to Allied efforts to defeat Germany on land. Almost all the British army's equipment was abandoned or destroyed, and a new army had to be rebuilt over the course of the following years. "Wars are not won", Churchill remarked on 4 June, "by evacuations".

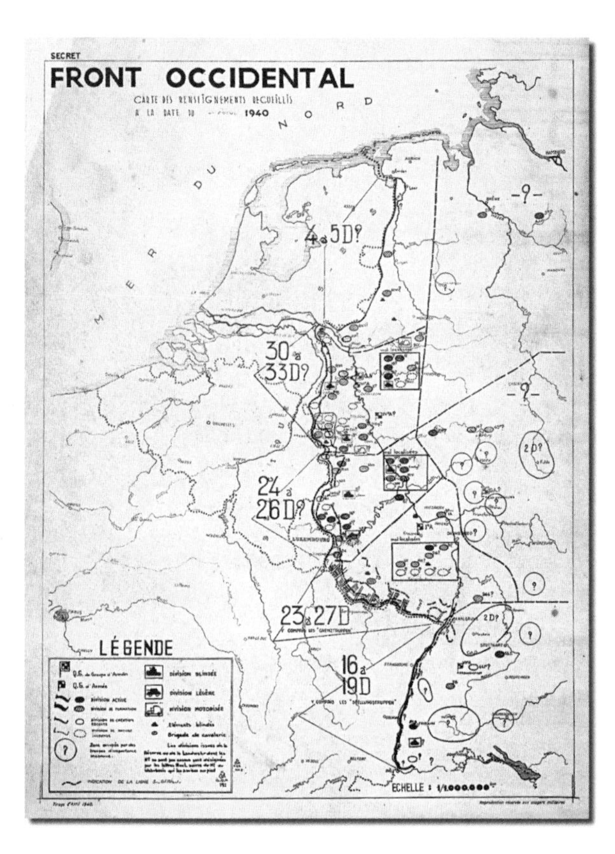

LEFT: A French map from 26 April 1940 setting out the French intelligence assessment of the German order of battle two weeks before the German attack.

ABOVE: French soldiers captured when the German army entered Dunkirk after the British evacuation, 4 June 1940.

BELOW: Shipping was an easy target for the German air force. Here the French destroyer *Bourrasque* is sinking off Dunkirk loaded with evacuees.

OPPOSITE, ABOVE: Motor vehicles on the quayside at Cherbourg during the evacuation, 13 June 1940.

OPPOSITE, BELOW: Troops arrive back at Dover from Dunkirk, 31 May 1940. In total around 228,000 British forces were rescued in nine days.

THE OTHER DUNKIRKS

Even as Operation "Dynamo" ended, there were more than 100,000 British troops still stationed in northern France, and as French resistance crumbled they fell back on the ports. On 13 June, 11,200 men were evacuated from Le Havre on the north French coast; 27,000 from St. Nazaire on 17–18 June. In total around 273,000 more British, French and Polish soldiers and airmen were evacuated to Britain between 13 and 25 June, a total not far short of the number saved at Dunkirk. On 17 June, a single German plane succeeded in hitting the overcrowded Lancastria in St-Nazaire harbour. The ship keeled over and only 2,477 of an estimated 6,000 crew and evacuees were saved. This was the worst disaster in British maritime history.

4–17 JUNE 1940
THE FALL OF FRANCE

The surrender of Belgium and the British evacuation from Dunkirk left France fighting almost alone against the German advance.

General Maxime Weygand, who succeeded General Gamelin on 19 May, organized an improvised defensive line along two rivers, the Somme and the Aisne, which had witnessed much of the fighting in the First World War. The German army reorganized into two major armoured spearheads led by von Kleist and Guderian, and attacked the Weygand Line on 5 and 9 June. After a few days of fierce fighting, the German forces reached the eastern edge of Paris. The capital was declared an open city, and on 14 June the German army entered almost deserted streets. The French government had fled first to Tours, where Churchill flew on 11 June to try to rally French resistance, then to Bordeaux. In the days before the German arrival, thousands of Parisians fled by car, train or on foot in what became known as *l'exode*, "the exodus".

Following the breakthrough to Paris, resistance began to crumble despite the existence of large units of the French army and substantial numbers of aircraft not yet defeated. German armoured forces pushed forward at high speed,

reaching Brest on the Atlantic coast by 19 June, Nantes by 20 June and as far as Bordeaux by 25 June, when the armistice, sought by the French government on 17 June and signed five days later, finally came into effect. In the east of France, the Maginot Line was penetrated in several places while German forces swung south to encircle what was left of the Second French Army Group under General Prétalat. French forces were forced to surrender piecemeal, but by 22 June French resistance towards the Germans was over.

On the Italian-French frontier in the south, however, hostilities continued. Mussolini declared war on France and Britain on 10 June, anxious not to miss any advantages he might gain from a peace settlement. Eleven days later, the 22 Italian divisions on the Italian-French frontier, totalling 300,000 men, were used to attack the southern French defences where they were held up by only six French divisions of approximately 85,000; the French strength had been greatly reduced following the redeployment of General Olry's forces to the north to face the German threat there. After four days of fighting, the Italians had gained almost nothing in the face of entrenched defences in difficult terrain. The Italian forces lost 1,258 dead and 2,631 wounded in the campaign; only 20 French soldiers were killed, and 84 wounded. On 24 June, an armistice was signed, ending what had been a brief, pointless and inglorious campaign. The battle to the north cost the French an estimated 90,000 dead and the loss of 1.9 million men as prisoners of war; German losses were 29,640 dead and 163,000 wounded.

For other Frenchmen the war continued beyond the armistice. On 6 June, the French premier, Paul Reynaud, had appointed the

ABOVE: French infantry surrender to the advancing German army in June 1940. Hundreds of thousands of French POWs were later made to work for the German war effort.

OPPOSITE: German troops parade through Paris following the occupation of the French capital, which was declared an open city on 13 June 1940 to avoid bombing attacks.

young General Charles de Gaulle as Under Secretary for War. He wanted to continue the fight and on 16 June encouraged Churchill to offer France a union of the two countries which he did with the backing of his cabinet. The French government refused, but de Gaulle smuggled himself out of France in an RAF aircraft and in London on 18 June made an historic appeal to a "Free France" to continue the fight against the German enemy. De Gaulle and the small number of supporters he gathered in England formally established the Free French forces on 7 August; they numbered only 2,240 officers and men. The newly formed Vichy government of Marshal Pétain declared them to be traitors but they formed the nucleus of what was to become a large and effective fighting force later in the war.

LEFT: Hitler standing at the Trocadero in Paris, in front of the Eiffel Tower, during his only visit to the captured city, on 28 June 1940. He was said to be delighted that Paris had been surrendered with its architecture undamaged by bombing.

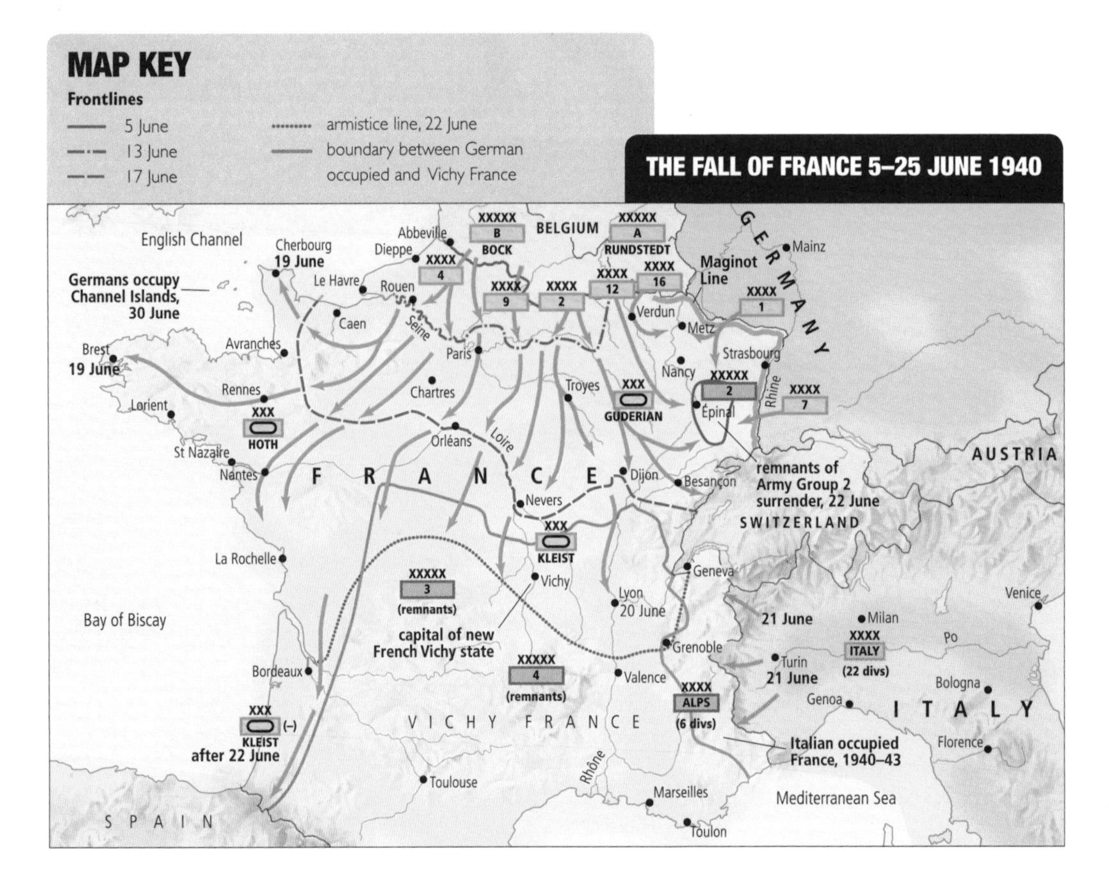

ABOVE: German poster of June 1940 celebrating their success in the west – "People of Germany! Your soldiers have, in just six weeks, after a heroic struggle, ended the war in the West against an intrepid opponent. Their deeds will go down in history as the most glorious victory of all time. In humility we thank the Lord God for his blessings."

RIGHT: General Charles de Gaulle seated at his desk in London, c.1940. He escaped from France during the evacuation and was recognized by the British government as leader of Free French forces on 28 June 1940. In 1940 he took part in an attempt to capture Dakar in West Africa from the Vichy regime.

JULY–OCTOBER 1940

THE BATTLE OF BRITAIN

On 18 June 1940, Winston Churchill told the House of Commons that "the Battle of France is over. I expect the battle of Britain is about to begin".

Over the following four months, the German air force attempted to destroy the RAF and undermine British military capability to an extent that would make the German invasion of southern England a possibility. It was the aerial duel fought out over the southern counties of Britain that became the Battle of Britain.

There were no clear dates for when the battle started and ended, but after it was over, an official Air Ministry pamphlet dated it from 8 August, when the air assault began to intensify and ended it on 31 October, when air attacks by German fighters petered out. German attacks began on 5–6 June, before the final defeat of France, and continued intermittently over June and July. These were probing attacks designed to lure Britain's RAF Fighter Command into combat and to destroy ports and communications. Only in August did the German air force commander-in-chief Hermann Göring order an intensified campaign following Hitler's directive, issued on 1 August, "to overpower the English air force". Air Fleet 2 under the command of General Albert Kesselring and Air Fleet 3 commanded by General Hugo Sperrle began a sustained attack on the airfields, supply depots and radar stations in southern England. By mid-August, Göring was confident that Fighter Command was on its knees and he ordered a final blow. The main attack was scheduled for Eagle Day (*Adlertag*) on 13 August, though poor weather on that day blunted the full scale of

the assault. Between 12 August and 6 September, there were 53 main attacks on airfields, all but two of them against the bases of No 11 Group led by Air Vice-Marshal Keith Park. The raids against radar stations were not sustained and only three of Park's airfields were put out of action and then only temporarily.

The German side assumed that the RAF was close to extinction, but the reality was very different. On 23 August, Fighter Command had an operational strength of 672 Spitfire and Hurricane fighters; by early September the figure was 738, more than at the start of the battle. Fighter Command losses totalled 444 aircraft between 6 August and 2 September; German losses were over 900 for the whole month, including bomber aircraft. Great attention had been paid by the Commander-in-Chief of Fighter Command, Air Marshal Hugh Dowding, to conserving RAF strength, training pilots and building reserves. Though hard-pressed in August and September, Fighter Command never came close to collapse. As the battle went on, it was the German air force that suffered levels of loss of aircraft and pilots that became in the end impossible to sustain. When Winston Churchill famously told the House of

ABOVE: When the approach of enemy planes was reported, RAF squadrons were "scrambled" to intercept them. Here pilots of No.19 Squadron, RAF based at Fowlmere in Cambridgeshire, are delivered by lorry to their waiting aircraft at the height of the battle.

OPPOSITE: The Supermarine Spitfire became the symbol of Britain's struggle in the air. Here a group of Mark IA Spitfires from No. 610 Squadron, based at Biggin Hill in Kent, fly in formation, July 1940.

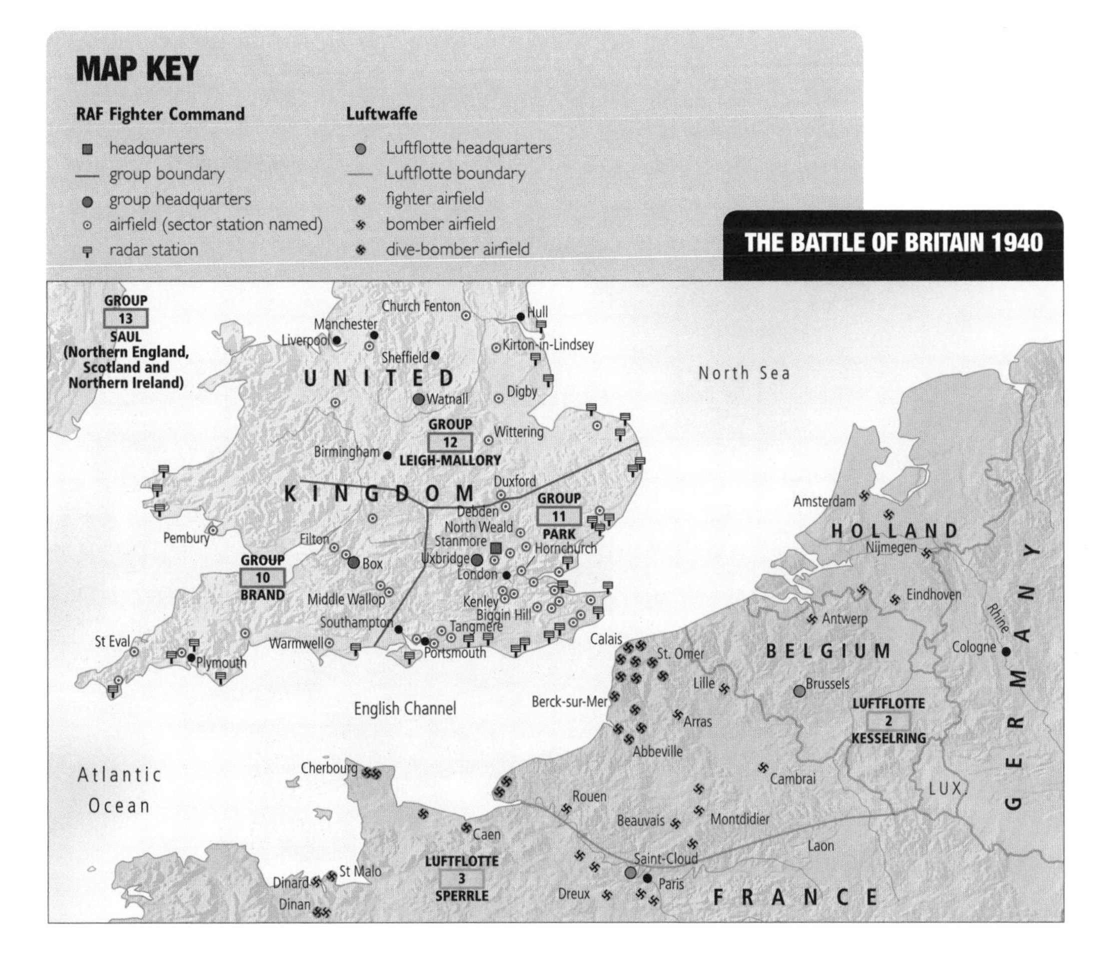

Commons on 20 August that "never in the field of human conflict was so much owed by so many to so few," he disguised the reality of a rising graph of British aircraft and pilot supply.

At the beginning of September, there came a sudden change in German tactics. The attack on the RAF was much reduced and German bomber fleets, escorted by large numbers of Messerschmitt Me109 fighters, were directed to attack London and other urban centres. Although the switch is often attributed to Hitler's desire to get revenge for RAF attacks on Berlin on the night of 25/26 August, it had already been planned on the assumption that Fighter Command had been destroyed. On 2 September, Göring ordered phase two of the attack, to destroy Britain's military and economic capability and demoralize the population prior to invasion. Hitler's speech on 4 September promising revenge was a propaganda stunt designed to make it look as if Britain had started the bombing. The switch in emphasis suited Fighter Command. It was now possible to attack the bombers as they approached London in large numbers and on their return, while German fighters were tied to protecting the slower and more vulnerable bombers and so less free to combat British fighters. In the first week of attacks, the German air force lost 298 aircraft, with 60 losses on 15 September, the day that has been celebrated ever since as Battle of Britain Day. Thanks to the survival of the radar chain, there was always advance warning of attack. British tactics were designed to maximize the damage to the attacking force and by the end of September it was clear to German commanders that they could not maintain the levels of attrition they were suffering. At the cost of only 443 pilots, Fighter Command inflicted losses of 1,733 aircraft on the German air force for the loss of 915 of their own. The conflict has gone down in British history alongside the defeat of the Spanish Armada in 1588 as one of the legendary moments in Britain's military past.

BELOW: A still from the camera-gun film of a Supermarine Spitfire Mark I as it attacks a formation of Heinkel He 111 bombers which have just bombed the Supermarine aircraft factory at Woolston, Southampton, 26 September 1940.

BELOW BOTTOM: Interior of the Sector "G" Operations Room at the RAF base at Duxford, Cambridgeshire, September 1940. The callsigns of the sqadrons operating out of Duxford are visible on the wall behind the operator third from left. On the extreme right are the radio operators in direct contact with the aircraft.

OPPOSITE: M.C.B. Boddington's Flying Log Book for 2 August–11 September 1940. He flew Spitfires throughout the Battle of Britain and then in Egypt and Malta during the campaign against the Italians. He shot down a total of 12 enemy planes.

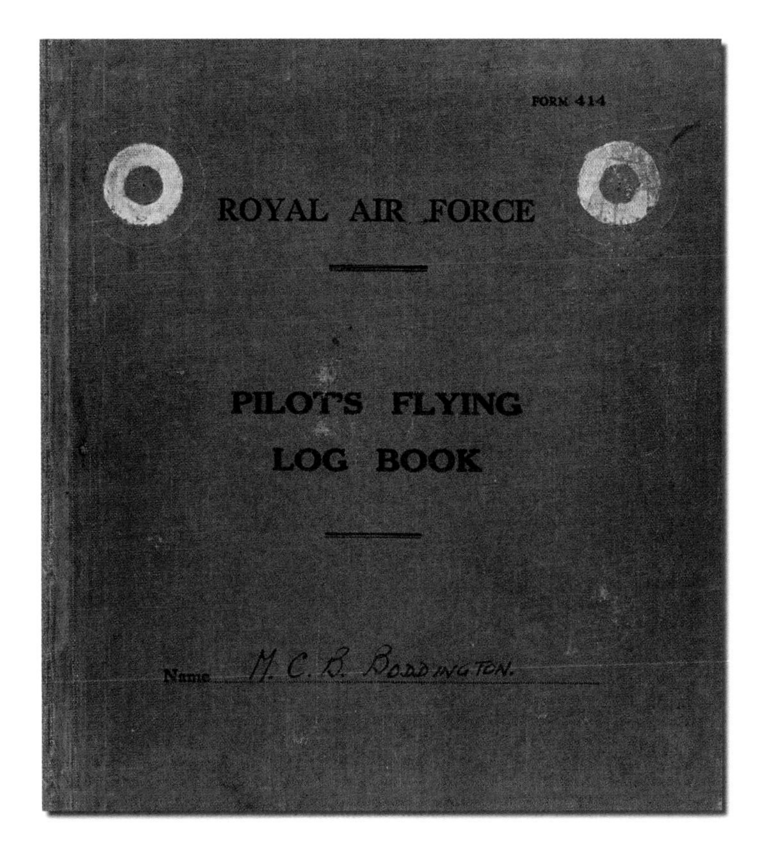
FORM 414

ROYAL AIR FORCE

PILOT'S FLYING LOG BOOK

Name M.C.B. BODDINGTON.

Year 1940 Month	Date	Aircraft Type	Aircraft No.	Pilot, or 1st Pilot	2nd Pilot, Pupil or Passenger	Duty (Including Results and Remarks)	Single-Engine Day Dual (1)	Single-Engine Day Pilot (2)	Single-Engine Night Dual (3)	Single-Engine Night Pilot (4)	Multi-Engine Day Dual (5)	Multi-Engine Day 1st Pilot (6)	Multi-Engine Day 2nd Pilot (7)	Multi-Engine Night Dual (8)	Multi-Engine Night 1st Pilot (9)	Multi-Engine Night 2nd Pilot (10)	Passenger (11)	Instr/Cloud Flying [Incl. in cols. (1) to (10)] Dual (12)	Instr/Cloud Flying Pilot (13)	Notes
—	—	—	—	—	—	— Totals Brought Forward	44.25	199.00		1.50	6.20	40.05		2.15	1.20		26.00			
August.	2.	Spitfire. U.		Self.		Scramble.		1.35												
"	4.	F.				Patrol base.		.40												
"	7.	X.				Scramble.		1.05												
"	8.	N.				Patrol. (2nd Channel "Blitz." 60 E/A down.)		.55												
"	"	N.				Return to base from Exeter.		1.30												
"	"	Magister.	3858			Dusk landings.		1.20												
"	9.	Spitfire. Y.				Scramble.		.45												
"	10.	Magister.	3868.			Night flying.		.50												Tail shot off one. 2nd attacked from beneath and S'bd side.
"	11.	Spitfire. T.				Patrol. (2nd Channel "Blitz" 61. E/A down)		1.25												Finished up 3 mls. N.E. of Wye in a stubble field. Hun pilot alive and set fire to machine. Should have fired him. Will do in future.
"	11.	Magister.	3858.			Night flying.		1.15												P/O Gordon. Killed. P/O Horton. Sgt Hornby. Shot down – Hun in sea – Ramsgate Bay. – Wounded.
"	12.	Spitfire. T.				Convoy patrol. 1st chase. Do. 215. Plymouth unconfirmed –		1.30												
"	12.	"	9819			Circuits + bumps.		1.15												7th S/Ld O'Brien. F/Lt Pat Hughes. Killed
"	13.	"	9819.			Scramble. Angels 10. to Pt. 7. ("Blitz" – 70)		.20												
"	14.	"	3280.			From St Eval to Middle Wallop		.50												
"	14.	"	"			Raid. 2nd chase. 1. Ju. 88 cotten. ("Blitz" – 20.)		1.10												
"	14.	"	"			"		1.00												
"	15.	"	9820			" ("Blitz" – 180)		1.00												
"	16.	"	9494			"		.15												Today 234 Sqdn returned to Home Base. Of those who set out
"	"	"	"			"														1 Month ago. The following failed to return.
"	"	"	"			"														S/Ld. O'Brien. Killed 7.9.40. P/O Horton. Wounded. 6.9.40.
"	18	"	"			"														F/Lt Pat Hughes. " 7.9.40. Sgt. Hornby. 6.9.40
"	"	"	"			"														P/O. Hight. " 15.8.40. P/O Lawrence. Posted. 603. 8.9.40.
"	21	"	3239			"														P/O Gordon Missing. 6.9.40. Sgt Bailey. " " 11.9.40
"	18	"	3283			To Hamble														P/O Hardy. Prisoner of War. 16.8.40.
"	"	Magister	3858	"	Sgt Harker	And return to the Wallop														P/O Parker. " " 16.8.40.
						Grand Total [Cols. (1) to (10)] 337 Hrs. 15 Mins. Totals Carried Forward	44.25	217.40		1.50	6.20	40.05		2.15	1.20		26.00			

5 AUGUST 1940–16 MAY 1941
THE EAST AFRICAN CAMPAIGNS

When Italy declared war on Britain on 10 June 1940, Mussolini hoped to be able to use the opportunity presented by Britain's preoccupation in Europe to mop up British territory in North and East Africa and create an enlarged Italian empire.

There were 326,000 Italian troops in Abyssinia in June 1940, 200,000 of them colonial troops (askari), supported by 244 mostly obsolete aircraft and 866 artillery pieces. They confronted a diffuse British Empire force, composed mainly of African recruits, numbering 40,000 supported by 100 mainly antique aeroplanes. In the first days of the British–Italian war, Italian forces occupied a number of towns on the border with Sudan and Kenya, and a force of 25,000 entered British Somaliland, compelling an evacuation of British Empire troops by 19 August to the British territory of Aden, on the Arabian coastline.

At this point, the Italian armies halted, giving the British commanders time to build up reinforcements from India, Nigeria, the Gold Coast (Ghana) and South Africa, including an invaluable squadron of South African Hurricane fighters, the most modern aircraft in the theatre. By the end of the year, there were 9,000 troops in Sudan, but in Kenya, which was to be the base for an invasion of Italian East Africa, General Alan Cunningham had

77,000 men, including 6,000 Europeans, supported by six South African air force squadrons. By November 1940, the British had cracked the Italians' codes and could read their plans and deployments almost immediately. In October, a force under the command of Brigadier William Slim began the campaigns with attacks on the Sudanese towns of Kassala and Gallabat, capturing the latter on 6 November. The full offensive was launched on 19 January by Lieutenant General William Platt, Commander-in-Chief Sudan, against northern Abyssinia, supported by two Indian divisions and a special unit known as Gideon Force made up of Abyssinian resistance fighters led by Major Orde Wingate, who, like Slim, was to become a famous name in the later campaign in Burma. After the heaviest fighting of the campaign in the mountainous region around Keren – where Italian forces held out for 53 days – Platt's army broke through, reaching the Eritrean coast at Massawa by 8 April.

In the south, General Cunningham launched a two-pronged attack from Kenya. The frontier town of Moyale was recaptured on 18 February by a small force designed to stimulate an Abyssinian revolt. The bulk of British Empire forces attacked on 11 February along the African coastline into Italian Somaliland. Although greatly outnumbered, the attack was a remarkable success. Mogadishu was captured on 25 February by the 23rd (Nigerian) Brigade, and the possession of the port allowed the 11th (East African) Division to link up with the move northwards into Abyssinia, amalgamating units from very different parts of Britain's African empire into a single fighting force. The inland city of Harar was captured in late March and Cunningham's force, joined by a seaborne invasion force from Aden which had landed on the coast on 25 February, reached the capital Addis Ababa on 6 April; there, following his triumphal entry on 5 May, the Emperor Haile Selassie was restored to the throne he had lost five years before. There remained large pockets of Italian forces in the mountainous regions of the country and these were gradually forced to capitulate by November 1941. The Italian commander, the Duke of Aosta, retreated to the region around the northern mountain city of Amba Alagi, where, short of weapons and supplies and with no hope of reinforcement, he surrendered on 19 May.

The British Empire victory was emphatic. For some 3,100 casualties killed and wounded, Allied forces captured 420,000 enemy troops and killed an estimated 12,000. Italian forces had suffered many disadvantages, for not only were their secret intelligence codes broken, but British naval power made it impossible to send supplies or reinforcements. Italian equipment was old-fashioned or ineffective: many artillery shells were left over from 1918 and failed to detonate. For an area almost as large as Western Europe, the Italians had only 6,200 vehicles, little fuel and 50,000 mules and horses. Above all, Italian forces were fighting for a cause for which they had little stomach against an enemy with higher mobility, more effective supply routes and complete dominance at sea and in the air. For British commanders, this was a vital area to secure for it prevented any threat to the Suez Canal area from the south and ensured that the long route to the Far East would not be threatened by any enemy presence in eastern Africa.

ABOVE: Aircrew of No.47 Squadron RAF change into flying suits outside their huts in Kassala, Sudan, in spring 1941 during the attack on Italian-held Ethiopia.

OPPOSITE: Italian Arab cavalry during the Italian capture of British Somaliland shortly before the withdrawal of British Commonwealth forces to Aden, 9 August 1940.

16 JULY–19 SEPTEMBER 1940

OPERATION "SEALION"

The defeat of France and the expulsion of British forces from mainland Europe presented Hitler with a quite unexpected opportunity.

German leaders assumed that Britain would see sense and find a way to end a conflict that could no longer be won. "We are very close to the end of the war," Joseph Goebbels, Hitler's Propaganda Minister, told his staff on 23 June. Hitler preferred a political solution and thought the idea of an invasion of Britain "very hazardous", but he decided in early July to explore both possibilities. On 7 July, the armed forces were instructed to begin preliminary planning for a possible invasion and on 16 July Hitler finally approved War Directive 16 for Operation "Sealion", the invasion of the south-eastern coast of England. This was to be a last resort if a political solution could not be found. On 19 July, Hitler made a peace offer in the German Reichstag. The speech was a celebration of German victory and Hitler made it clear that he would discuss terms "as a conqueror", but he also assured the British that he had no desire to destroy the British Empire. If war continued it would, Hitler concluded, be Britain's choice.

In Britain there had been talk since late May in some political circles of reaching a compromise peace but Churchill was irrevocably committed to fighting on and that became the official position. Hitler's speech was almost disregarded, evoking a brief rebuttal by Lord Halifax, the Foreign Secretary, on 22 July. German leaders found the British position hard to understand, but on 23 July the German press were officially informed by the government that the war would continue. At Hitler's headquarters, Operation "Sealion" now became a serious option, though it soon became clear that there were many barriers to its operational feasibility. The German navy, whose commander-in-chief, Grand Admiral Raeder, had been among the first to suggest invasion to Hitler in June, remained hesitant over recommending a hazardous

cross-Channel operation against British air power and the Royal Navy. The destruction of the RAF was a priority without which invasion was regarded as too risky.

The tentative date set for a landing was 15 September. The invasion plan was for six divisions from the 9th and 16th armies to invade on a broad front from Hythe in Kent to Newhaven and Rottingdean on the Sussex coast. The armies would then move rapidly inland, supported by the German air force, to reach a preliminary line running from Gravesend to Portsmouth, and after capturing London to a second line between the Essex coast and the Severn Estuary. Barges and small boats were gathered from all over occupied Europe to ports along the French, Belgian and Dutch coasts and intensive training in beach assault undertaken over the summer. Bomber Command kept up a relentless attack on the invasion ports which added to the many difficulties of organizing a large-scale maritime invasion, something that the German armed forces had done only against light resistance in Norway, and then at great cost in shipping losses. On 30 August, with no clear sign that the Royal Air Force had been defeated, the invasion date was switched to 20 September. In Britain expectation of invasion marked the whole of September. On 7 September, the codeword "Cromwell" was issued to all units to be on full alert. The weekend of 14–15 September was widely regarded as the most likely date and as troops moved into position along the coast they were ordered to sleep with their boots on. When nothing happened, the full alert was dropped, to be reinstated on 22 September. Only in late October was the signal "invasion improbable" sent out to units.

On the German side, there were mixed feelings about the risk of invasion. Defeat would not have been disastrous but would have been politically unfortunate. At a meeting on 14 September, with British forces at full alert and the RAF undefeated, Hitler announced that although preparations were complete, the invasion of Britain was too risky. He proposed a review two days later for possible landings on 27 September or 8 October, but the situation had not improved. On 19 September, the preparations were ordered to be scaled down and the invasion shipping was dispersed from the vulnerable North Sea ports. On 12 October, Hitler finally ordered "Sealion" to be dismantled. Fear of the Royal Navy and the failure to dent British air power rendered invasion impossible. Hitler ordered a sustained air attack on British cities in case the British government could be terrorized into surrender.

OPPOSITE: Royal Artillery gun crews run to man a 9.2inch- (23.5cm) gun during a practice shoot at Culver Point Battery, Isle of White, 24 August 1940.

ABOVE: A fighting column from the South Wales Borderers in a training exercise in Bootle, Liverpool, 16 August 1940. All over the country soldiers prepared for the threatened German invasion.

RIGHT: A flotilla of destroyers at Scapa Flow in 1942.

7 SEPTEMBER 1940–16 MAY 1941

THE GERMAN BLITZ ON BRITAIN

The heavy bombing of British cities began with an attack on London on 7 September 1940.

Bombing had been conducted intermittently against ports and other military and economic installations since June. In July, 258 civilians had been killed; in August 1,075. The first attacks on the London area began on 18/19 August and on central London on the night of 22/23 August. A heavy attack took place on Liverpool on 28/29 August. The attack on 7 September, however, was the first to be carried out in response to Hitler's orders issued on 5 September to

destroy the industrial, military and supply systems of the capital. The 350 German bombers who attacked the docks in east London two days later initiated what became known in Britain as "the Blitz".

The German plan was to degrade Britain's capacity to wage war and to undermine the war-willingness of the population, but once the invasion plans were suspended in mid-September, the attacks assumed a more directly political purpose. German leaders hoped that the attacks on cities would force Britain to negotiate and make invasion unnecessary, and on 16 September Göring ordered the new phase of city bombings to begin in earnest. Up to 5 October, there were 35 major air assaults, 18 of them against London, and all conducted in daylight. Unsupportable loss rates forced the German air force to switch to night bombing, and from early October until 16 May 1941, German aircraft attacked a wide range of major cities on nights when the weather conditions permitted. The air units were instructed to attack specific targets and they were helped in this by a system of radio navigation beams known as *Knickebein* which worked effectively until British scientists found ways to jam the German beams during November and December 1940. During the campaign German aircraft also used navigation systems known as *X-Gerät* and *Y-Gerät* but these too became subject to increasingly effective jamming.

The Blitz was concentrated on London, which was attacked for 57 days in a row between 7 September and 2 November and then regularly until 10 May. The most famous day of the Blitz was the night of 29 December when a large part of the City of London was destroyed by 136 German bombers. It was on that night that the symbolic photograph was taken of St Paul's Cathedral rising above the flames and smoke. The Blitz was also directed at most British ports and industrial centres, from Belfast in Northern Ireland, to Glasgow in Scotland and, to Plymouth (which was heavily bombed between 21 and 23 April 1941), Southampton and Portsmouth in the south. The raid that provoked the widest publicity was that on Coventry on the night of 14/15 November 1940 which killed 554 people. In the major raids on London, 18,800 tons of bombs were dropped; in major attacks against other cities the total was 11,800 tons. The bombing killed 43,000 people and destroyed or damaged one million houses, but did little serious or long-term damage to the British economy or military effort.

OPPOSITE: Londoners shelter in Aldwych underground station, 8 October 1940, one of 79 stations used as deep shelters. Several were hit during the Blitz, causing heavy casualties.

ABOVE: The London Fire Brigade at Eastcheap in the City of London. By the end of 1940 around 20,000 incendiary bombs had been dropped on the capital.

LEFT: A wrecked bus standing in the ruins of Coventry, heavily bombed on the night of 14/15 November 1940. The city became a symbol for the horror of the Blitz and later established close links with the German city of Dresden, destroyed in February 1945.

OPPOSITE, ABOVE: General Sir Frederick Pile (right) watches the firing of Britain's "rocket gun" on the South West Coast, 1944.

OPPOSITE, BELOW: A panorama of the city of Liverpool after heavy bombing raids in 1940. The River Mersey is visible to the left of the photograph, the Liver Building in the centre.

GENERAL SIR FREDERICK PILE (1884–1976)

A career artillery officer who rose to the rank of major in the First World War, Frederick Pile was a gifted organizer and a keen modernizer. He played an important part at the War Office between 1928 and 1932 in planning the mechanization of the armed forces. After a brief period in Egypt, he returned in 1937 to command the London 1st Anti-Aircraft Division. On 28 July 1939, he was appointed commander of the Anti-Aircraft Command, a post that he filled throughout the war, the only senior commander to do so in the British army. He reorganized Britain's anti-aircraft defences, expanded the supply of guns and shells and when labour shortages took men away, he recruited 74,000 women into the anti-aircraft ranks. After the war he took up a business career.

The British response focused on both active and passive defence. By May 1941, there were 16 squadrons of night fighters which became more effective as the battle wore on but found it difficult to locate the bombers without sophisticated detection devices. There were 1,785 heavy and light anti-aircraft guns in the summer of 1940, and over 4,500 searchlights, though these too were of limited effectiveness. A high proportion of German losses during the Blitz came from accidents to crews flying long distances in poor weather conditions. The passive defences were organized country-wide by more than two million volunteers of the Air Raid Precautions organization, including evacuation and the distribution of gas masks. By 1940, around 2.5 million cheap Anderson bomb shelters – named after Sir John Anderson, responsible for Civil Defence measures – had been produced for householders and in every city deep concrete bunkers were constructed or cellars and underground facilities converted. Nevertheless, civilian casualties were high and in many of the most heavily attacked cities there was an exodus from the threatened area and evidence of demoralization and rising crime levels. The government made many concessions, which included the use of parts of the London Underground network as improvised air-raid shelters, and domestic morale stiffened as the Blitz continued. When it finally ended in May 1941, Britain was more, rather than less, determined to continue to fight.

JUNE 1940–MARCH 1941

NAVAL WAR IN THE MEDITERRANEAN

When the war opened in the Mediterranean in June 1940 the balance of forces between the *Marina* Italiana and the Royal Navy was strongly in Italy's favour.

Italy needed to be able to control the sea in order to ship supplies and military resources to its North African empire, which was to be the take-off point for an attack towards the Suez Canal. The Royal Navy needed to be able to interrupt Italian supply lines while at the same time keeping open its own routes from Gibraltar in the west, via Malta and Cyprus to the naval base at Alexandria and the Suez Canal in the east.

The effectiveness of surface vessels was compromised by the use of submarines and aircraft, both of which took a heavy toll of naval and merchant shipping during the war. In the Mediterranean the traditional heavy battle fleet was exposed to permanent danger unless it could be protected by effective air cover. This lesson was driven home by two operations conducted by the British fleet in November 1940 and March 1941 which effectively neutralized any threat posed by the

large Italian surface fleet. The first operation, codenamed "Judgement", was an attack by naval aircraft on the major Italian naval base at Taranto, on the southern coast of the Italian peninsula. It was the brainchild of the Mediterranean fleet carriers' commander, Rear-Admiral Lumley Lyster, who arrived in September 1940 at Alexandria aboard the carrier HMS *Illustrious*. He had already prepared a contingency plan for just such an attack when he had been a captain in the Mediterranean in 1938 and the Fleet Commander, Admiral Andrew Cunningham, responded to the revived plan enthusiastically. Originally scheduled for Trafalgar Day, 21 October, it was postponed until 11 November because of a fire on board the carrier. In the interval Mussolini launched a war against Greece, which gave a British attack a greater sense of urgency.

Of the two carriers available only *Illustrious* took part since HMS *Eagle* had been damaged by bombing. The attack was undertaken by Fairey Swordfish torpedo bombers, old bi-planes with open cockpits, but very effective in the absence of air defence. Two waves of 12 and nine aircraft were launched, two of each wave instructed to drop flares to illuminate the area and then attack the port installations. Good reconnaissance had given warning of barrage balloons and protective netting, and both were avoided. The two waves seriously damaged three battleships for the loss of two aircraft. The Italian navy immediately ordered all units to withdraw to safer harbours on the more distant western coast. The major new battleship *Vittorio Veneto* was unscathed but she was damaged in a second operation against the Italian fleet mounted four months later, in March 1941.

The second engagement, the Battle of Cape Matapan, was a direct result of the war in Greece. German pressure on Italian forces to interrupt the flow of British supplies and reinforcements brought a reluctant Italian naval high command to plan an operation around the battleship *Vittorio Veneto* to surprise and destroy an escorted British convoy to Greece. The Royal Navy could break Italian codes and were warned in advance of the Italian move. Convoys were suspended and a mixed force of carriers and battleships converged on the Italian force. The battle again highlighted the importance of air power at sea. The Italian battleship was hit by a torpedo in the second wave of attack by Albacore torpedo bombers, but was able to limp away to safety. Confused intelligence combined with Admiral Cunningham's reluctance to mix his battleships with the air pursuit of the Italian fleet resulted in losses less severe than they might have been. Nevertheless the cruiser *Pola* and a number of smaller Italian ships were sunk and the operation to interrupt British convoys defeated. The Italian fleet never again sought a fleet encounter, and the war against the Royal Navy was now conducted by aircraft and submarines. This was a lesson not lost on the Japanese navy. Taranto was a rehearsal for the later devastating attack on Pearl Harbor.

OPPOSITE: The most powerful Italian battleship, *Vittorio Veneto*, played a central role in the Battle of Cape Matapan.

ABOVE: Admiral Sir Andrew Cunningham, Commander-in-Chief of the Royal Navy's Mediterranean Fleet. He was an acting Admiral until his rank was confirmed following Taranto.

RIGHT: An aerial reconnaissance photograph of the damaged warships at Taranto on the morning after the attack by the Fleet Air Arm on the base, 12 November 1940.

MERS-EL-KÉBIR

After the French defeat in June 1940 the fate of the powerful French fleet was a source of anxiety for the British, who did not want German or Italian control of French ships. Under the terms of the Franco–German armistice the French fleet was to be immobilized under their supervision, although some French naval units were in British territory. Britain acted to pre-empt any prospect of Vichy France handing over its vessels to the Axis. On 3 July 1940 all French ships in British ports were seized, and a Royal Navy group, Force "H", under the command of Admiral James Somerville, was sent to the French naval base at Mers-el-Kébir to negotiate with the French commander for the destruction, handing over or immobilization of the French naval forces stationed there. When British requests were refused Somerville opened fire, destroying the battleship *Bretagne* and damaging a number of other ships. Vichy France broke off diplomatic relations and made a brief attack on Gibraltar in retaliation, but the threat of the French fleet was effectively removed.

OPPOSITE: Fairey Swordfish Mk I torpedo bombers on a training exercise from Crail in Scotland. The slow bi-planes proved very effective against targets where there was no effective air cover.

RIGHT AND BELOW: The Royal Navy aircraft carrier HMS *Illustrious* in the Mediterranean. The right-hand photograph shows the ship under attack from the German air force. The stationing of the German aircraft in the Mediterranean in 1941 led to a sharp increase in shipping losses.

7 DECEMBER 1940– 9 FEBRUARY 1941

OPERATION "COMPASS": DEFEAT OF ITALY IN NORTH AFRICA

With the outbreak of war between Italy and Britain on 10 June 1940, it seemed certain that the large Italian forces concentrated in the colony of Libya – more than 236,000 – would be used to threaten the British position in Egypt where, under the terms of the 1936 Anglo-Egyptian treaty, Britain had stationed air, naval and land forces.

Control of the Suez Canal was the Italians' final objective, which, if achieved, would open up supply routes to their beleaguered forces in East Africa. Not until 13 September did Mussolini order the Italian army forward. The five divisions of the Italian 10th Army, led by General Mario Berti, greatly outnumbered the two poorly equipped mobile divisions available for the defence of Egypt under the command of Major General Richard O'Connor. Italian forces advanced 95km (60 miles) into Egyptian territory, and then dug in along a defensive line from Sidi Barrani on the coast.

The Italian failure to press forward into Egypt gave British Empire forces time to consolidate and to absorb the new supplies of Matilda tanks and other equipment arriving from Britain. With the permission of the Commander-in-Chief Middle East, General Archibald Wavell, O'Connor undertook a risky large-scale raid – codenamed Operation "Compass" – to try to push the Italian front back. On 8 December, the Indian 4th Division infiltrated the loosely-held Italian defensive line while the 7th Armoured Division skirted round the Italian line

LEFT: Gloster Gladiator fighters of the Royal Australian Air Force flying over the mobile operations room on a landing ground near Sollum in Egypt used during Operation "Compass".

OPPOSITE: Port installations burning in Tobruk, 24 January 1941, two days after British and Commonwealth troops had captured the town. Italian tanks are in the foreground with a white kangaroo symbol to show they have been captured by Australian forces.

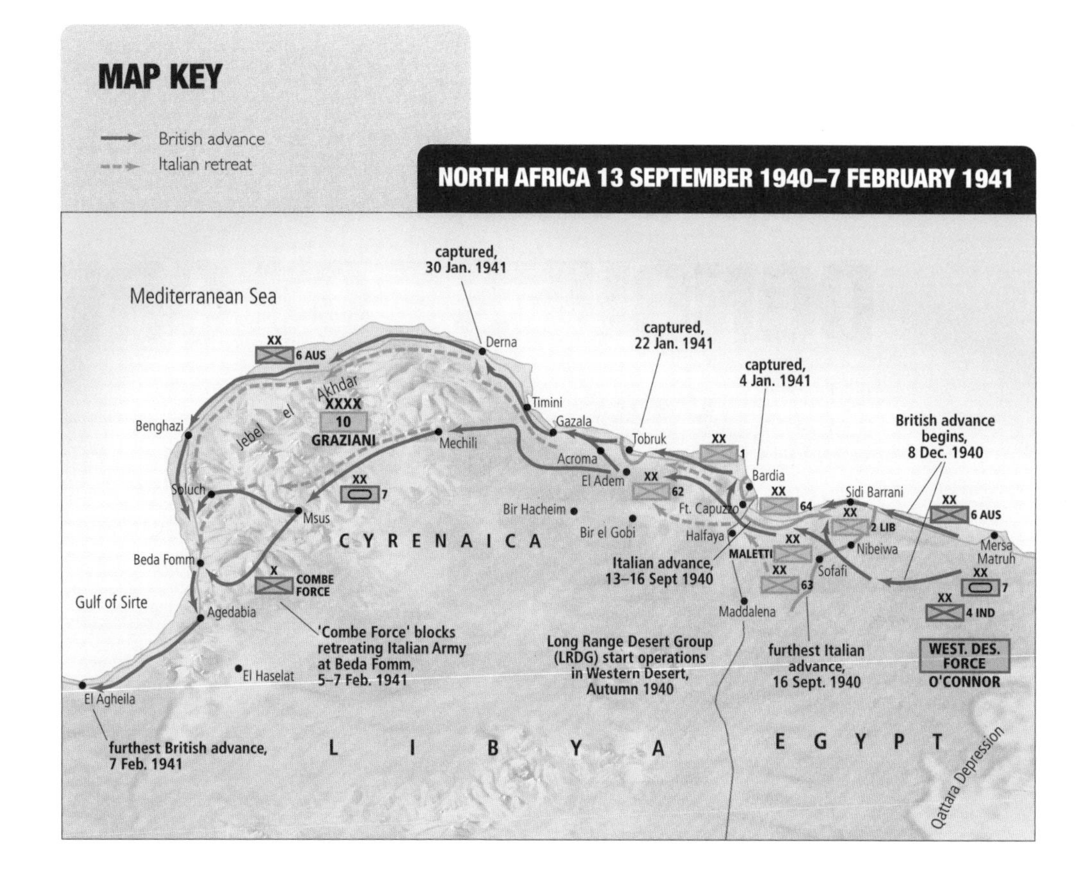

and attacked it from the rear. The Italians broke and over 38,000 prisoners were taken. The rapid success of the raid encouraged O'Connor to move on to invade the eastern Libyan province of Cyrenaica, the Australian 6th Division pursuing Italian forces along the coastline, while the 7th Armoured again pursued a wide sweep towards the port of Tobruk. After stiff fighting, the Libyan port of Bardia fell on 4 January, and on 22 January Tobruk was captured, denying the enemy an important supply base.

The Italian army under Marshal Graziani was pulled back to the defence of Tripolitania, the western province of Libya, where the first German reinforcements arrived to shore up Italian resistance. British Empire forces pushed on rapidly, until by early February almost all of Cyrenaica was in their hands. A long trek across the desert by 7th Armoured, who arrived on 5 February at Beda Fomm near the coast of the Gulf of Sirte just half an hour before the retreating Italians, succeeded in cutting off their line of escape. After a brief conflict the Italian army surrendered on 7 February, while British Empire forces pressed on to El Agheila, where their attack came to a halt. Reinforcements had to be transferred to the Balkan campaign in an effort to stem the Axis assault on Greece, which left behind only a light force in North Africa. However, for some 2,000 British Empire casualties, around 30,000 Allied troops had routed an army eight times their size. Over 130,000 Italians were taken prisoner, and those who returned to Tripolitania needed extensive re-equipping. In six months the Italian empire in Africa had suffered defeats from which the Italian war effort never effectively recovered.

20 MAY–3 JUNE 1941

THE GERMAN CONQUEST OF CRETE

With the expulsion of British forces from mainland Greece, Hitler was anxious to complete the campaign by capturing the island of Crete which would otherwise remain a potential base for air attacks on the German flank or against oil targets in Romania.

He ordered the rapid capture of Crete. Operation Mercury was prepared at great speed and was based around the deployment of Germany's elite paratroop force, XI *Fliegerkorps*, heavily protected by the German air force. The campaign was launched on 20 May, just three weeks after the expulsion of British Empire forces from southern Greece.

The defenders of Crete were a mixed force of British, Australian, New Zealand and Greek troops which numbered around 35,000, substantially more than the attacking force. They were commanded by Lt General Bernard Freyberg, a British-born New Zealander with a reputation for fearlessness. Though large in numbers, the force lacked adequate artillery, tanks or communications equipment. The one advantage Freyberg enjoyed was ULTRA intelligence information. He was the first field commander to be given this secret intelligence, which indicated the precise date of the German attack. He disposed his forces around the three key airfields on the north coast at Maleme, Retimo and Heraklion, but the force was spread very thin. When General Kurt Student's paratroopers descended on 20 May, they faced fierce resistance and suffered heavy casualties, but after a parachute battalion under Colonel Bernard Ramcke landed on either side of the airfield on the morning of 21 May, Maleme fell to a determined German assault, allowing German transport aircraft to bring in General Julius Ringel's 5th *Gebirgs* (Mountain) Division. Hitler was disillusioned at the high level of losses during the initial paratroop assault and Student was forced to give way to Ringel for the conquest of the rest of Crete.

The battle hung in the balance for several days. On 21–22 May, a German convoy bringing reinforcements from Milos was mauled by a Royal Navy force with the loss of around 5,000 men. But German air superiority was gradually achieved and the Royal Navy lost three cruisers and six destroyers, with damage to 17 other vessels, almost all from air attack. By 23 May, German forces deployed on Crete had increased from 9,500 on the opening day of the operation to 17,500, and Freyberg's forces were pushed back to the south of the island, with small pockets holding out in Retimo and Heraklion, aided by Cretan guerrillas whose attacks provoked a savage series of reprisals against the civilian population. By 26 May, Freyberg reported that he could no longer hold the island and over the next four days the Royal Navy evacuated most of the garrison, the last ship leaving in the early hours of 31 May. Around 5,000 men were left behind, most of whom went into German captivity; a small number escaped into the hills with the Cretan partisans or found small ships to take them to Egypt after the main force had left. The ships plying back and forth between Alexandria and Crete were subjected to regular bomb attack; of the 3,700 British Empire dead, 2,000 were from the Royal Navy.

OPPOSITE, TOP: Wounded soldiers disembark at an Egyptian port after evacuation from Crete, 31 May 1941. This was Britain's fourth major evacuation in a year of fighting.

OPPOSITE, BELOW: German paratroopers and Ju52 aircraft over Crete, May 1941. The German force took very heavy casualties and was never used in an invasion role again.

For the German forces the conquest of Crete was a pyrrhic victory. The German dead numbered 3,352, of whom 1,653 alone were from Student's XI *Fliegerkorps*. Total casualties were 6,698, which exceeded losses for the whole of the Balkan campaign in April. Almost 200 transport aircraft were destroyed during the operation, denying valuable resources to the imminent invasion of the Soviet Union. General Freyberg was not given an independent command after Crete, but he did lead the New Zealand Corps in Italy, and later became Governor-General of New Zealand; but Kurt Student was never again trusted by Hitler, even though Crete had been a significant victory completing German domination of Europe.

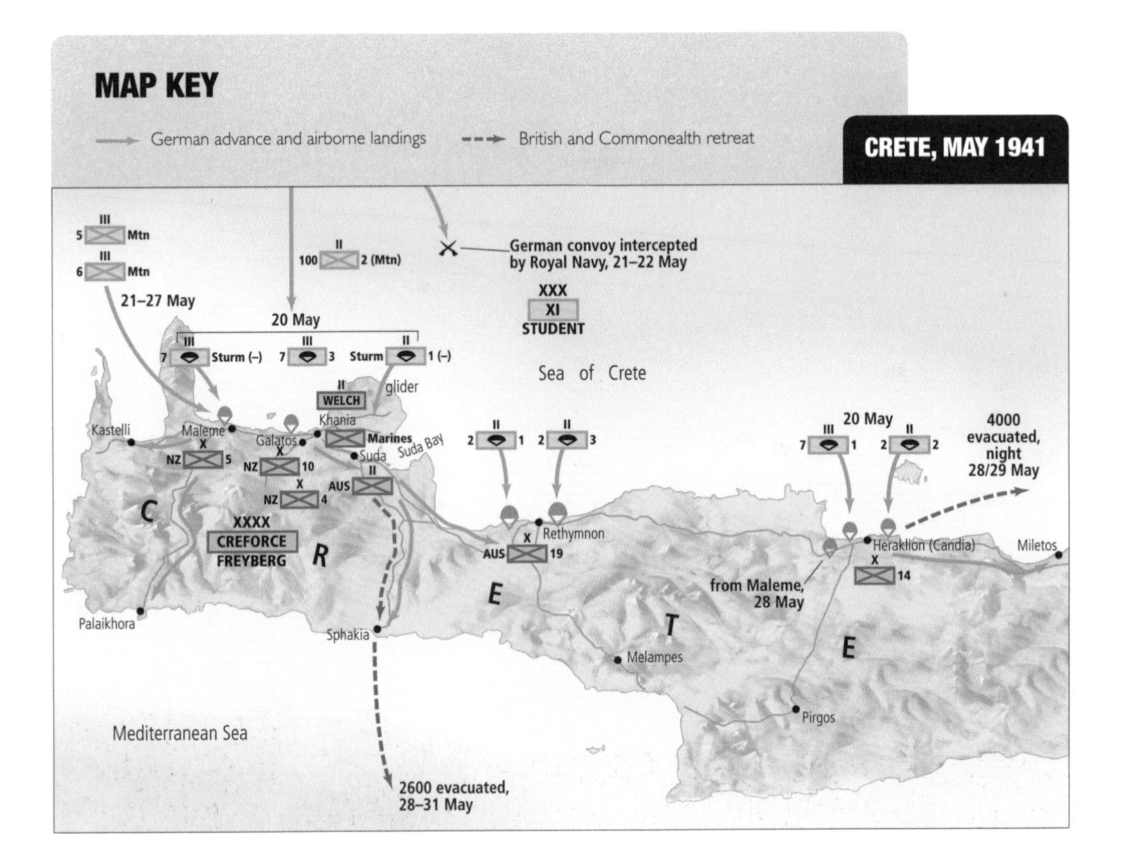

GENERAL KURT STUDENT (1890–1978)

Kurt Student is usually regarded as the founder of modern paratroop forces. An airman in the First World War, he developed an interest in gliding during the 1920s which he used when developing Germany's first airborne unit, *Fliegerdivision* 7, in 1938. He was promoted to Inspector of Airborne Forces later in 1938, and in 1940 his men played a key role in the invasions of Norway and Belgium. His plan for the invasion of Crete backfired with heavy losses and Hitler refused to let Student use mass airborne assaults again. His forces were largely confined to ground operations and Student ended the war as Commander Army Group Vistula in May 1945. After the war, he was tried by the British in May 1947 for war crimes and though found guilty on three counts the verdict was not upheld. Britain denied a Greek application for his extradition to stand trial for atrocities against Greek civilians, which Student had ordered as reprisals against partisan attack. Student was freed on medical grounds but lived on to the age of 88.

OPPOSITE ABOVE: The commander of the British Commonwealth forces on Crete, Lieutenant General Bernard Freyberg, watches the German advance from his dugout. He was retired from the army in 1937 on grounds of poor health, but was brought back in 1939 and commanded the New Zealand Expeditionary Force in the Mediterranean theatre.

RIGHT: Two British ships burning in Suda Bay in Crete, May 1941, after an attack by German bombers of XI *Fliegerkorps* stationed in Greece.

BELOW: A series of three photographs taken by a German airman of the sinking of HMS *Gloucester* off Crete, 22 May 1941. British ships took heavy losses from German aircraft stationed in Greece.

24–27 MAY 1941

SINKING THE *BISMARCK*

All the evidence from the first 18 months of the war showed that the traditional role of naval vessels had been subverted by the arrival of air power.

The German navy, however, persisted with plans for a large battle fleet and failed to build the aircraft carriers which were now essential to give surface ships effective protection. The most up-to-date and largest German battleship was the 41,000-ton *Bismarck*, launched on 14 February 1939 and commissioned on 24 August 1940. The ship was intended as a convoy raider in the Atlantic, and her design reflected this, with a broad beam to cope with heavy seas and large fuel tanks. The break-out into the Atlantic, codenamed Operation "Rhine Exercise", was planned to include the battlecruisers *Gneisenau* and *Scharnhorst* and the new battleship *Tirpitz*, but the first two were damaged or under repair and the *Tirpitz* was still engaged in trials before full commissioning. The original force would have been a formidable fleet, but in the end *Bismarck* left on 18 May 1941 accompanied only by the heavy cruiser *Prinz Eugen*.

The commander of the operation, Vice Admiral Lütjens, had reservations about its feasibility but he obeyed commands to the letter, anxious not to be sacked like his predecessor, Vice Admiral Wilhelm Marschall, for disobeying orders. The British were forewarned of the break-out through ULTRA intelligence and from Swedish and Norwegian sources. The ship was spotted by a Spitfire reconnaissance aircraft near Bergen, but contact was not made until 23 May, when the German units entered the Denmark Strait between Iceland and Greenland and a radar-equipped heavy cruiser, HMS *Norfolk*, detected them. The force was shadowed until heavier British ships became available. Early in the morning of 24 May

1941, the new British battleship *Prince of Wales* arrived, accompanied by the battlecruiser *Hood* commanded by Vice Admiral Lancelot Holland. Within minutes, *Hood* had been hit by accurate German gunfire, and at 6.00 a.m. blew up and then sank in three minutes with the loss of all but three of the 1,418 crew. Captain Lindemann aboard *Bismarck* wanted to pursue and destroy the *Prince of Wales*, which had also sustained serious damage, but Lütjens obeyed his instructions not to engage heavy enemy units and insisted on moving on. *Bismarck* had also been damaged: the forward radar was not operational and the fuel tanks were leaking, forcing her to reduce speed to 20 knots. *Prinz Eugen* made off into the Atlantic while *Bismarck* made for the French coast at St Nazaire for essential repairs.

The British shadowed the battleship, but a sudden turn by *Bismarck* confused the pursuers and contact was lost. Only Lütjens's insistence – against Lindemann's advice – on sending a half-hour radio message, which was duly intercepted by the British, gave a clue to the ship's whereabouts, but the pursuing battleship *King George V* miscalculated the position and the German ship drew closer to air cover and destroyer assistance from France. But on 26 May, a Catalina flying-boat of Coastal Command spotted *Bismarck* and at 9.00 p.m. that evening a Swordfish torpedo-bomber from the carrier *Ark Royal* succeeded in scoring a hit that jammed the rudder and steering equipment. On the morning of 27 May, the British battleships *Rodney* and *King George V* moved in for the kill, bombarding a slow and listing target and, just after 9.00 a.m., destroying the bridge and eliminating the ship's command. The final sinking is usually attributed to the torpedoes of the destroyer HMS *Dorsetshire* which fired three at the *Bismarck* shortly before the ship sank, at 10.39 a.m., with the loss of all but 100 of more than 2,000 crewmen. Recent research of the wreckage and the testimony of survivors have suggested that the German battleship was scuttled rather than sunk by the enemy. The end of *Bismarck* epitomized Grand Admiral Raeder's gloomy hope, expressed when war broke out, that his men would understand "how to die gallantly" in what he always viewed as an unequal struggle with the Royal Navy. In reality, it was one aircraft that succeeded in slowing down and disabling *Bismarck*, further testimony that the days of traditional fleet engagements were now in the past.

OPPOSITE: Able Seaman Alfred Newall aboard the cruiser HMS *Suffolk*. He was the first to sight the *Bismarck* as she emerged into the Denmark Strait.

ABOVE TOP: The *Bismarck* on fire on 27 May 1941, photographed from one of the Royal Navy vessels shadowing her last hours.

ABOVE: A Fairey Swordfish returns to the aircraft carrier HMS *Ark Royal* after making a torpedo attack on the *Bismarck*. The attack damaged the rudder and steering and sealed *Bismarck*'s fate.

24 MARCH–17 JUNE 1941

DEFEAT IN NORTH AFRICA

On 12 February 1941, General Rommel arrived in the Libyan port of Tripoli to command a German expeditionary force, the Afrika Korps, which had been sent by Hitler to shore up the collapsing Italian position in North Africa.

Although ordered to behave cautiously, he immediately took advantage of the weakening of British Commonwealth strength caused by the diversion of resources to the Greek campaign. On 24 March, he launched an attack together with the Italian Ariete and Brescia divisions against the weakly held line at El Agheila, and by 31 March was ready to advance across Cyrenaica in defiance of orders from Berlin. He organized mobile Axis units into three lines of attack: the Italian armour advanced along the coast towards Benghazi, while two German columns moved across the desert to cut off the Allied position.

The campaign was an exceptional success. The British abandoned the defensive line in central Cyrenaica on 6 April, and their two commanders, General Neame and General O'Connor, were captured by an Axis patrol on 7 April. By 8 April, Italian and German forces met at the coast and pressed on to Tobruk, where the Australian 9th Division had retreated. Tobruk was under siege by 11 April, but all attacks were repelled and the city remained besieged until December, reinforced by convoy to prevent its surrender. By this time the German High Command was anxious that Rommel not over-commit his forces and General Paulus was sent to order him in person to hold a defensive line west of Tobruk at Gazala. This order was transmitted to Berlin and intercepted and deciphered by British intelligence. Churchill was keen to use this information to launch a counter-attack and ordered General Wavell to use new supplies of tanks and aircraft, delivered by the "Tiger" convoy, to carry the battle back to Rommel. By this time, in defiance of Paulus, the Afrika Korps had reached Bardia and Sollum, close to the Egyptian border.

LEFT: A gun of the Royal Horse Artillery firing at German forces on the perimeter of the Libyan port of Tobruk during the campaign for the city in 1941.

OPPOSITE: German air-force base in Cyrenaica during the campaign in 1941. Junkers Ju 52 transport aircraft (on the ground and in the air) were the backbone of Rommel's airborne supply system. In the foreground are Me110 twin-engined fighter bombers.

FIELD MARSHAL ERWIN ROMMEL (1891–1944)

Rommel was the most famous of Hitler's generals. A dedicated and effective commander, he was a soldier's soldier, daring and tough and willing to share the dangers of his men. A career soldier who fought with distinction in the First World War on the Western and Italian fronts, he was a champion of fast, mobile warfare and commanded a Panzer division in the campaign in France. He was made a General in January 1941 and sent to command the Afrika Korps, a formation set up to support Italian forces in the Western Desert. In June 1942, he was made Germany's youngest Field Marshal, but his force was defeated in North Africa in May 1943. He helped organize the German defence of northern France but was wounded in an aircraft attack on 17 July 1944. Implicated in the bomb plot against Hitler three days later, he chose suicide rather than face a trial for treason.

The British Commonwealth counter-attack, Operation "Brevity", began on 15 May against German forces at Sollum. The campaign made little headway, and by 27 May German forces had recaptured the ground temporarily lost. Wavell was under pressure to act and on 15 June launched a second counter-attack, Operation "Battleaxe", which was even less successful in penetrating the Axis line at Bardia. The Afrika Korps used the 88mm anti-aircraft gun as anti-tank artillery to devastating effect. Having blunted the Allied attack, Rommel's forces pushed on towards Egyptian territory to end the threat from a demoralized enemy. On 17 June, British forces withdrew into Egypt to defend the Suez Canal. Rommel's forces dug in to a defensive line at Sollum, having recaptured almost all of Cyrenaica in a lightning two-month campaign.

Wavell was relieved by Churchill on 1 July and replaced with General Claude Auchinleck as Commander-in-Chief Middle East. By this time the British Commonwealth forces and support troops in the Middle Eastern theatre numbered over one million men, and represented the largest combat theatre command in existence, with an airforce of 49 squadrons and over 700 aircraft. Auchinleck resisted Churchill's efforts to go over to an early offensive, preferring to build up substantial reserves and equipment before running the risk that a premature assault like "Brevity" and "Battleaxe" would bring a third defeat. Throughout the desert campaigns Egypt was virtually taken over by the British: large transit and training centres were set up, oil pipelines constructed, water pipes laid from the Nile into the desert, and new roads and air bases constructed, most of it using Egyptian labour. The British presence was accepted reluctantly by many Egyptians, and British commanders knew that they faced not only a formidable military foe, but the possibility of political instability in the rear.

8 JUNE–14 JULY 1941

THE ALLIED INVASION OF IRAQ & SYRIA

With German forces in the Balkans and pressing forward in the Western Desert, British leaders became anxious that the position of British interests in the Middle East, particularly oil, which was vital for the whole war effort in the Mediterranean, might be threatened by a combination of Axis military success and pro-Axis sympathy among the Muslim populations of the Middle East.

Plans were discussed as early as March 1940 for possible action in Iraq where anti-British nationalism was a threat to the Mosul oilfields; Operation "Sabine" was prepared for the possible transfer of troops from India to Basra. When Iraq's regency was overthrown by a military coup in early April 1941, the British ambassador, Sir Kinahan Cornwallis, who arrived in Baghdad in the midst of the coup, urgently requested British military intervention before the anticipated arrival of German aircraft and troops.

On 17 April the first Indian troops arrived in Basra and two days later 400 men of the 1st King's Own Royal Regiment flew in to reinforce the Habbaniya air base near Baghdad. The rebel leader, Rashid Ali, decided to destroy the British military presence and on 1 May the Iraqi army began to dig in around the air base to prepare to capture it, hoping that their action would bring German support. The British commander of the base, Air Vice-Marshal Smart, decided to fight and on 2 May, before Iraqi forces were ready, launched a heavy air attack against them. The Iraqi air force of 56 largely obsolete aircraft was soon halved in strength and relentless bombing forced retreat from the perimeter of the base. A relief force was organized from Trans-Jordan codenamed "Habforce", under the command of Major General John Clark. Out of almost 6,000 troops, a rapid-movement column of 2,000 was created to reach the air base quickly. By this time around 25 German aircraft were available from Iraqi and Syrian airfields to help the rebels. The advance column was attacked by German bombers, but reached Habbaniya on 18 May.

By this time Iraqi resistance was crumbling. The forces available at the air base moved out to Fallujah on 19 May, captured the town and moved on Baghdad. German air forces were outnumbered and 21 aircraft destroyed. On 30 May, Iraq's five-division army abandoned the fight and an armistice was signed. The Regent returned to power in October and on 17 January 1943 Iraq declared war on the Axis. The help given to Rashid Ali from bases in Syria, a French mandate loyal to Vichy France, prompted Churchill to authorize a further operation to secure the Middle East for the Allies. On 23 June, an operation under the command of Lieutenant General Maitland Wilson was launched against the Vichy French in Lebanon and Syria from Palestine in the south and Iraq in the east, using "Habforce" and the 10th Indian Division, which had been landed at Basra during May, as well as the Australian 7th Division. Slow progress was made against the French garrisons, but by 6 July the 7th Australian Division began the battle for Beirut, which followed the occupation of Damascus on 21 June. The commander of Beirut capitulated on 10 July and the Vichy authorities signed an armistice (the Acre Convention) on 14 July. Some 32,300 French troops were repatriated and Syria was placed under British military control until its independence in 1946. Wilson remained in the area, commanding what was now called Ninth Army against the risk of a German thrust from the north through the Soviet Caucasus. The two campaigns secured a vital area that combined Britain's war effort in Europe and Asia and frustrated further Axis advance.

OPPOSITE: British soldiers on 12 July 1941 comb the ruins of the Temple of Baal, near Palmyra in Syria, for Arab snipers employed by the Vichy French regime to obstruct the British advance.

RIGHT: Arab legionaries guard a landing ground beside the Iraq Petroleum Pipeline in Trans-Jordan, where a group of Gloster Gladiator fighters are refuelling. The aircraft were on their way from Egypt to help the besieged airfield at Habbaniya in Iraq.

MAP KEY

oilfields
Vichy advance
British advance
French advance
Soviet advance
Iraqi advance

THE MIDDLE EAST APRIL–AUGUST 1941

TURKEY
Diyarbekir
Euphrates
Tigris
Tabriz
Ardebil
Caspian Sea
Rasht
Qazvin
Teheran
occupied, 17 September
Mosul
Luftwaffe units arrive, 15 May
Kirkuk
Aleppo
Raqqa
10 IND
Cyprus
Nicosia
Latakia
SYRIA
Deir Ez Zor
Homs
Vichy forces surrender, 3 July
Luftwaffe units arrive, 12 May
HABFORCE
Hamadan
Qum
VICHY
Palmyra
Abu Kemal
Tekrit
Kermanshah
PERSIA (IRAN) (neutral)
Invaded by Allies to secures supply lines to USSR, 24–25 August
Beirut
LEBANON
Damascus
Tyre
Merjuyan
KINGSCOL
Ramadi
Baghdad
Habbaniya
Fallujah
IRAQI
7 AUS
FREE FRENCH
1 CAV
HABFORCE
Vanguard force
Jerusalem
IRAQ
PALESTINE
Allies invade Vichy territory, 8 June
Commonwealth detactment relieves Habbaniya, 18 May
Iraqi forces surround British airfield
Amara
Indian division secures oilfields
EGYPT
TRANSJORDAN
Euphrates
Bandar Shahpur
Basra
10 IND
Aqaba
SAUDI ARABIA
KUWAIT
Kuwait
Persian Gulf

18 NOVEMBER 1941–21 JANUARY 1942

OPERATION "CRUSADER"

The failure to dislodge Rommel's Afrika Korps from the Egyptian frontier in the summer of 1941 led to one of the few periods of static warfare in the Desert War.

Rommel and his Italian allies created a defensive line around the towns of Sollum and Bardia, while the newly-appointed General Auchinleck refused to bend to pressure to attack the Axis until he could be certain of a preponderance of force. While the army built up its strength, the RAF Western Desert Air Force, under the overall command of Air Chief Marshal Arthur Tedder, kept up a relentless bombing of German positions, including 100 attacks on the port of Benghazi and 70 attacks on Tripoli. Tedder organized new tactics of close support for the army with standing fighter patrols linked by radio to army liaison units to permit quick battlefield response, a lesson learned from German practice. The army's Western Desert Force (renamed the 8th Army on 18 September 1941) was strengthened, so that by November 1941 it numbered 118,000 men, drawn from British, New Zealand, South African and Indian forces. The Axis were outnumbered in tanks (680 to 390) and even more in aircraft (1,000 to 320). Auchinleck planned a major campaign, Operation "Crusader", to win back Cyrenaica and to lift the siege of Tobruk. When the moment came to attack, German forces were in the process of preparing yet again to attack Tobruk and remove the threat to the long Axis flank.

"Crusader" began with mixed fortunes: Allied forces moved forward on 18 November, meeting stiff resistance. The attempt by the Tobruk garrison to break out and meet

the XXX Corps as it advanced west across the desert was broken by Rommel, who had begun to retreat back towards Tobruk once he realized the scale of Auchinleck's plan. The Italian forces were abandoned at Bardia and Sollum, where they surrendered only after fierce resistance on 2 and 12 January respectively. German counter-attacks south of Tobruk around Sidi Rezegh produced a chaotic battlefield, and at one point Rommel ordered his remaining tanks to drive for the Nile Delta, thinking that enemy armour was all but annihilated. The commander of the Allied force, Lieutenant General Sir Alan Cunnigham, the victor in East Africa, uncertain about his position, requested permission to retreat. Auchinleck replaced him with his deputy chief of staff, Acting Major-General Neil Ritchie, who stabilized the operation. The XXX Corps linked up with the Tobruk garrison, threatening to cut off Axis forces. Rommel instead retreated westwards in good order on 8 December, while Allied forces entered Tobruk on 10 December, lifting at last the 240-day siege. By this time the town was no longer defended by the Australian troops who had

OPPOSITE: In a scene more reminiscent of the London Blitz, British searchlights and anti-aircraft fire light up the night sky above the Egyptian port and British naval base of Alexandria. Bomb bursts from Axis aircraft attack can be seen in the background.

ABOVE: Officers of the Royal Horse Artillery in Tobruk at the unit's command post, 1 November 1941. One officer is watching where the shells land while the other is shouting fire orders through a loudhailer. The siege of Tobruk was lifted by 10 December.

occupied it in the spring, but by a mixture of British, Indian, South African and Polish forces, including the Polish Carpathian Brigade.

Rommel was pursued across the territory won earlier in the year. Gazala, Benghazi and Mersa Brega all fell again to Allied forces, who by the end of 1941 had travelled 475 kilometres (300 miles) and recaptured the whole of Cyrenaica. After Soviet defeats and the onset of quick victories for Japan in the Pacific, the advance in Libya was an important morale boost for the embattled Allies. The victory, however, proved to be a hollow one. Rommel retreated with his undefeated Afrika Korps back to El Agheila, where he could regroup and exploit the fresh supplies which were landed at Tripoli in January. Once these reached the front line he prepared to push back the British Commonwealth forces, by now overstretched and short of supplies. Auchinleck failed to appreciate his enemy's true position and planned a new campaign, Operation "Acrobat", to seize the western Libyan area of Tripolitania. On January 21, Rommel pre-empted him by launching what was to prove a devastating riposte to the apparent success of "Crusader".

ABOVE: Acting Major-General Neil Ritchie, commander of the British 8th Army from December 1941 until he was sacked in the summer of 1942 after Rommel had succeeded in driving his forces back across the territory won in Operation "Crusader".

LEFT: A British Matilda tank and truck in the desert at the start of Operation "Crusader". British Empire and Commonwealth forces had a superiority of two to one in tanks by the time the battle started.

OPPOSITE: German forces advance in the area between Tobruk and Sidi Omar. The battles during Operation "Crusader" flowed back and forth across the desert until Rommel's decision to withdraw on 8 December once it was clear that he was outnumbered.

FIELD MARSHAL CLAUDE AUCHINLECK (1884–1981)

Apart from a short period in 1940 in Norway and then as chief of Southern Command in England, Claude Auchinleck spent almost all his military career outside Europe. A career soldier, he served in the Middle East during the First World War and subsequently in the Indian Army. He was recalled to Europe as a major general, commanded British forces in Norway, and then returned to Britain to head up 5th Corps, where he was involved in organizing the Home Guard. In November 1940, he was appointed Commander-in-Chief in India, and then on 5 July 1941 Commander-in-Chief Middle East, by which time he was a full general. His mixed performance against Rommel in 1941–42 led Churchill to remove him from office in August 1942. He returned to India in June 1943 as Commander-in-Chief, a post he held until 1947. He was promoted field marshal in 1946.

8 DECEMBER 1941–11 MAY 1942

BLITZKRIEG IN ASIA AND THE FALL OF SINGAPORE

The Japanese attack on Pearl Harbor was planned to coincide with a number of complex and daring combined operations to seize Southeast Asia, the East Indies and a string of small islands in the western Pacific to secure supplies of oil, rubber, tin and other minerals, and to discourage the British and American governments from attempting the difficult and expensive task of recapturing the new southern zone of the Japanese Empire.

Within four months the vast area of the European powers' empires in the Far East was under Japanese rule.

On 7 December, a Japanese seaborne striking force under General Tomoyuki Yamashita assembled in the Gulf of Siam destined the following day to occupy the Kra Isthmus in southern Thailand and to assault the British airfields in northern Malaya. Other strike forces prepared to seize Hong Kong, assault the Philippines, and then conquer the British and Dutch possessions in the East Indies. The campaign was an extraordinary success. In Malaya Yamashita commanded around 60,000 men, but defeated a British Empire force more than twice as large. The attempt by the Allied army to hold up the Japanese advance was half-hearted at best. By 9 January, the Japanese were almost at the Malayan capital of Kuala Lumpur. Adept at jungle warfare and tactics of infiltration, the Japanese army proved an irresistible force against a poorly prepared enemy with limited air power. By 31 January, Malaya had been abandoned and the British forces were withdrawn to the island of Singapore.

Japanese progress in the Philippines was less spectacular. The northernmost island of Batan was occupied on 8 December and the main island of Luzon assaulted by seaborne forces two days later. Further out in the Pacific, small islands were seized to prevent any threat from the central ocean area. The US base at Guam was occupied on 10 December. The garrison on Wake Island resisted the first Japanese attack on 11 December, but succumbed to a larger air and sea assault 12 days later. The attack on the East Indies, defended by Dutch, British, Australian and colonial troops, began a week later on 15 December with landings on the island of Borneo. In a daring series of combined operations the Japanese army swarmed out over the archipelago, targeting airfields and oil installations. One branch of the assault moved southeast to capture the British Solomon Islands. Admiral Takahashi's task force concentrated on driving through the central zone, taking Bali on 19 February and Timor the next day. The capital of the Dutch East Indies, Batavia (Jakarta), was captured on 5 March. Japanese warships and aircraft hunted down surviving Allied shipping and destroyed it, although some of the Allied force was evacuated to Australia from Java, harried by Japanese aircraft. On 19 February, to drive home the Japanese success, bomber aircraft destroyed a large part of the northern Australian port of Darwin. The Dutch surrendered on 9 March, the rest of the Allies three days later.

Japanese plans worked almost like clockwork. There was no intention of creating a larger campaign area than their limited forces could protect and Australia was safe for the present. In the Indian Ocean the British naval presence, weakened by the sinking of HMS *Prince of Wales*

TOP: Japanese soldiers of General Yamashita's force storm a British-held village during the rapid conquest of Malaya. In seven weeks a larger British Empire and Commonwealth force was relentlessly driven back by an army whose soldiers were regarded in the West as racially inferior.

LEFT: British prisoners being marched into captivity in the British colony of Hong Kong following a brief resistance in December 1941. Thousands of British and Empire prisoners perished in Japanese camps and labour service during the war.

ABOVE: RAF American-made Brewster Buffalo fighters flying over Malaya.

LEFT: A stream of British army vehicles fleeing from the Japanese invasion of Malaya on their way to the island of Singapore across the bridge over the Straits of Johore which linked the island with the mainland.

BELOW: Lieutenant General Percival (far right) leads the British surrender party to meet Japanese negotiators on 15 February 1942. This was the largest military force to surrender in British history and it astonished the Japanese, who had expected greater resistance.

and HMS *Repulse* on 10 December, was challenged by a daring raid led by Vice Admiral Nagumo, whose task force attacked Colombo in Ceylon on 5 April 1942, then the naval base at Trincomalee, sinking four warships, including the carrier *Hermes*, the first to be sunk by carrier aircraft. There was no intention yet of extending the Japanese Empire into the Indian Ocean area, but simply the aim to undermine the delicate British political position in southern Asia and to warn Britain to stay at arm's length from the new Japanese Empire which had been established across thousands of miles in the space of little more than four months.

The loss of Singapore was the largest and most humiliating defeat suffered by British Empire forces throughout the Second World War.

The island of Singapore was the major British naval base in the Far East and the hub of the defence of British possessions in the Pacific. It

had been reinforced during the interwar years by the addition of heavy guns pointing seaward to ward off any possible invasion by a naval force. The rapid invasion of the Malay Peninsula in December 1941 and January 1942 by Lieutenant General Yamashita's 25th Army upset all the plans for the defence of Singapore. On 31 January, the evacuation from Malaya to Singapore across the Strait of Johore was completed. The British commander, Lieutenant General Percival had to face an attack from the north against a coastline which had not been effectively prepared for major defensive action.

Percival had under his command around 70,000 troops, mainly Indian and Australian. A British formation, the 18th Division, arrived just before the Japanese attacked but played only a small part in the subsequent battle. Yamashita could muster around 35,000 troops supported by substantial numbers of aircraft. To meet the expected assault, Percival deployed his forces in a broad but light covering line along the coast, too weak to hold a sustained assault and lacking any mobile reserve force to help repel a landing. On the night of 8/9 February, Japanese forces landed in strength, soon broke the defensive line and drove in two waves towards the city of Singapore. After the long retreat through Malaya the British Empire forces had exaggerated respect for the Japanese enemy and a growing sense of hopelessness about the battle. By 12 February, the Japanese had reached the city itself, around which Percival had thrown up a primitive defensive screen. Retreating soldiers began to panic and a stream of deserters and refugees added to the confusion in the attempt to defend the central districts.

Fighting for the city proved more determined nonetheless. Yet after three days of resistance, with Yamashita's supply lines under growing pressure, Percival bowed to his fellow officers' view that further resistance was a pointless waste of lives. On the afternoon of 15 February Percival surrendered along with an estimated 100,000 British Empire troops and officials, some of whom had arrived only to experience almost immediate imprisonment. Many of the 45,000 Indian troops were invited to join the Indian National Army inspired by the radical nationalist Subhash Chandra Bose. By August 1942, only around 15,000 had refused to join. The 50,000 European and Australian prisoners were taken to Changi camp in the north-east of Singapore Island and thousands of them later died in the work projects on mainland Asia. Their mistreatment arose partly from the Japanese military ethic which deplored surrender; Yamashita and his officers were astonished that 70,000 men could surrender against a much smaller force without showing greater determination to fight. Japanese casualties from the campaign amounted to only 1,714 killed.

For the civilian inhabitants of Singapore there followed several years of victimization and mass murder. An estimated 30–50,000 were killed, including not only many from among the Chinese population but also ethnic Malays suspected of criminal activities, anti-Japanese sentiment or communist sympathies. The term used by Chinese to describe these activities by the Japanese military and secret police was *sook ching* or "purification by elimination". Singapore then became one of the major centres of the Japanese southern empire. It was renamed Shonan ("Light of the South") and became the headquarters of the Southern Army. When Yamashita surrendered to the Americans in Manila in 1945, Percival, recently freed, was invited to witness the signing.

RIGHT: The surrender negotiations at the headquarters of Lieutenant General Yamashita (seated, centre) in the Ford Works Building in Singapore. The Japanese commander insisted on immediate and complete surrender.

3 MARCH 1941–27 MARCH 1942

COMMANDO RAIDS: NORWAY TO ST NAZAIRE

In the summer of 1940, Churchill ordered the creation of a number of small units for raiding the enemy coast in Europe.

The initial 11 battalion-size groups were known as Commandos; each comprised 500 men who were highly trained for the dangerous task of breaching the German-held coastline and inflicting local damage or securing vital intelligence. No. 2 Commando would later become the Parachute Regiment. A Royal Marines officer, Lieutenant General Alan Bourne, was appointed Commander of Raiding Operations, charged with using the commando units for organized raids, but he was replaced almost at once by Admiral Roger Keyes. The first operations were minor raids in June and July 1940, but by 1941 the force was sufficiently prepared to begin more ambitious projects.

The most successful operations were mounted against the northern Norwegian Lofoten Islands on 4 March and 26 December 1941. The first of these netted valuable information to help crack the German navy's "Enigma" codes. The second was designed as a diversionary attack while another raid took place against the Vaagsö Islands in central Norway, on 27 December, where a small force, supported by naval gunfire, destroyed military installations and communications and captured 100 Germans for the loss of 19 commandos.

Larger and more significant raids were planned for the French coast at Bruneval and St Nazaire. Both were carried out under the new adviser on Combined Operations, Lord Louis Mountbatten. The first landing, on the night of 27/28 February, was designed to seize material from the new German Würzburg radar which was used to control night fighters against British bombing attacks. The raid at Bruneval, near the French port of Le Havre, was mounted by a paratroop unit, which overcame the local German garrison, took parts of the radar and returned to Britain successfully across the Channel. The second

OPPOSITE: A commando of the Newfoundland Heavy Artillery Regiment on a training exercise in Britain in 1942. Commandos were given a tougher regime of preparation than the normal soldier and were all volunteers.

ABOVE: British commando troops on the quayside watch an oil installation burning during their raid on the Norwegian island of Vaagso on 27 December 1941.

RIGHT: Badges for the Combined Operations forces created in the Second World War to carry out raids on enemy territory.

LORD LOUIS MOUNTBATTEN (1900–79)

A great-grandson of Queen Victoria, Louis Mountbatten joined the Royal Navy in the Great War, and had risen to the rank of captain by 1937. He was an ambitious, charming and flamboyant personality though an ineffective naval commander. In October 1941, Churchill appointed him as adviser on Combined Operations. In April 1942, he was promoted to vice-admiral and chief of Combined Operations with orders to undertake raids on the enemy coast, and he organized the raids on Bruneval, St Nazaire and later Dieppe. In October 1943, he became Supreme Commander, South-East Asia Command where he organized the defence of Imphal against the Japanese. After the war he became the last Viceroy of India. He was assassinated by the IRA while on a fishing trip in 1979.

attack, against the French port of St Nazaire, was a larger and more dangerous operation designed as part of the Battle of the Atlantic which was reaching its height in the summer of 1942.

St Nazaire, on the French Atlantic coast, had the only dry dock large enough for the German battleship Tirpitz, which it was feared would use the base to raid Allied merchant shipping. An American-built destroyer, Campbeltown, made available to the British under the September 1940 destroyers-for-bases deal, was packed with explosives in its bow, and on the night of 27/28 March was sailed into the French harbour under the

ABOVE: Men of "C" Company, 2nd Parachute Battalion, returning on a motor torpedo boat to Portsmouth on the morning following the Bruneval raid, 28 February 1942. The commander of the assault force, Major J D Frost, is on the bridge, second from left.

LEFT: A wounded commando being helped back to the landing craft during the operation against Vaagsö. Combined operations depended on close work between the army and navy to ensure effective evacuation from missions with a high degree of risk.

range of German guns. The destroyer avoided detection and rammed the dock's outer wall. A force of 268 commandos stormed the dock and destroyed equipment. The following day, five tons of explosive blew up the dock wall, killing the Germans who had gone on board the destroyer and two captured Commando officers (who had revealed nothing about the impending explosion). The raid took a heavy toll on the force – 611 took part, of whom 397 were caualties, including 144 killed – but the damage done was severe enough to justify the attack.

The success of the commando operations was mixed, but they became a regular feature of British warfare, a useful source of intelligence and a growing irritation to the German High Command. Following a raid on the Channel Islands on 3 October 1942, in which a number of bound German soldiers were killed, Hitler ordered that British and Canadian prisoners should be placed in shackles. On 18 October he issued a decree that any British commandos or special forces caught on raids were no longer to be treated as regular prisoners-of-war but were to be handed over to the German security forces for interrogation and punishment. The shackles were removed after the British had responded in kind on German prisoners, but Hitler's Commando Order stayed in place

ABOVE: The destroyer HMS *Campbeltown* crashed into the sluice gate in St. Nazaire harbour on the night of 27/28 March 1942. It was loaded with explosives, which blew up shortly after this photograph was taken, destroying the sluice-gate.

ABLE SEAMAN WILLIAM SAVAGE VC

Able Seaman William Alfred Savage was awarded the Victoria Cross for his part in the St Nazaire Raid. He was aboard a motor gun boat (MGB) in charge of a pom-pom gun and during the attack on the port engaged enemy shore-fire and shipping even though his position was completely exposed to enemy fire. He was killed at his gun and was one of three naval personnel to be awarded the decoration as a result of the raid.

APRIL–AUGUST 1942
THE SIEGE OF MALTA

The island of Malta, some 95 kilometres (60 miles) from the coast of Sicily, was home to a medium-sized British naval base midway between Gibraltar and the Suez Canal.

The island had a small but vociferous Italian community which had campaigned during the 1930s for the island to become part of the new Italian empire, and it was a prize that Mussolini coveted when he declared war on Britain on 10 June 1940. The following day Italian aircraft bombed the island, beginning an ordeal of aerial siege that was to last over two years.

Although the Italian navy had developed plans for the seizure of Malta as early as 1935, a frontal assault was regarded as costly, despite the fact that in June 1940 there were only three obsolescent Gloster Gladiator biplanes to defend the whole island. Nicknamed "Faith", "Hope" and "Charity", they were sent up to engage the Italian bombers. Of the trio, "Faith" succeeded in surviving the entire siege. Malta remained a thorn in the Axis side, but not until January 1941, when the Italian air force was reinforced with a German Fliegerkorps X based on Sicily, did intensive bombing begin the systematic destruction of much of the above-ground targets in Malta. In July 1941, an Italian naval flotilla attempted an unsuccessful attack on the harbour at Valetta, Malta's capital. During the course of the year, it proved possible to keep Malta supplied and a flow of munitions, aircraft, food and medicine made its way on the dangerous convoy routes into the island.

In December 1941, heavy bombing began again, in support of Axis operations in North Africa, with continuous attacks by German and Italian aircraft. Between 1 January and 24 July 1942, there was only a single day on which bombs did not fall. This was a period of exceptional hardship for the island population, which was forced to live a subterranean

OPPOSITE: An aerial view of Operation "Pedestal" in August 1942, when a small number of merchantmen, heavily escorted by warships of the Royal Navy, arrived in Malta. In the foreground are the carriers HMS *Victorious*, *Eagle* and *Indomitable*.

RIGHT: Soldiers and civilians clear up the damage in Kingsway, the principal street in the Maltese capital of Valetta, after air attack in April 1942. During the siege a large part of the city and its surroundings was destroyed.

BELOW: Maltese resistance came to depend on the supply of the high-quality Spitfire fighter. Here RAF fitters and Maltese civilian workers repair damaged Supermarine Spitfire Mark Vs in a maintenance shed at Ta Kali.

existence for much of the time, short of food and medical supplies. The first half of 1942 was a difficult time for the British war effort in the Mediterranean. A combination of Axis air power, minefields and submarines threatened to end the British presence in the region, while by June 1942 Rommel had succeeded in pushing the British Commonwealth forces back into Egypt. The decision to hold on to Malta made increasingly less sense as its capacity to strike back by sea or air was progressively undermined. In May 1942, the German Commander-in-Chief, Field Marshal Kesselring, announced that Malta was now neutralized, but by July, now under the command of Lord Gort, Malta once more had operational Spitfire fighters and operational submarines.

The month before, the island had been awarded the George Cross by the British king, the highest decoration for civilian bravery in recognition of the suffering it had endured; over the course of the siege there were 5,257 civilian casualties, including 1,540 deaths. By now, the siege was almost complete: in March 1942, just three merchant ships arrived at Malta out of a convoy of only four, shielded by 28 Royal Naval vessels. Two convoys sent from Gibraltar and Alexandria to relieve the island in June 1942 were able to bring only two merchant ships through, for the loss of six naval vessels and six merchantmen. Close to starvation, the population was saved by the arrival of the "Pedestal" convoy in August which lost nine out the convoy of 14 but brought five into Valetta harbour. Allied victory at El Alamein and the conquest of Axis air bases in North Africa brought the siege effectively to an end by November, despite Kesselring's decision to inflict a further round of heavy bombing on the battered island in October. A few weeks later, in Operation "Torch", American and British forces landed in Algeria and Morocco, and the Mediterranean became a major theatre of war.

20 JANUARY–16 JUNE 1942

JAPAN CONQUERS BURMA

The conquest of most of Burma by Lieutenant General Shojiro Iida's Japanese 15th Army in the first five months of 1942 represented the furthest limit of Japanese westward expansion.

Burma became important to Japanese planners as a means to interrupt the flow of resources along the "Burma Road" to the Chinese armies they were fighting and to the area already conquered in Southeast Asia with its rich material resources. Burma also possessed oil and significant supplies of the rare metal tungsten. Later, it was to be a possible stepping stone for the invasion of India.

Burma's sudden strategic significance was understood far too late by the British authorities who controlled the country in conjunction with a Burmese native administration established under the Burma Act of 1935. Many leading Burmese politicians were anti-British and pro-Japanese, and the nationalist Burma Independence Army, an organization of Burmese dissidents, waited in the wings. In late 1941,

there were around 27,000 British and Empire troops in Burma, 15,000 of whom were Burmese, organized into frontier forces and the 1st Burma Division formed in July 1941. The great bulk of remaining forces were Indian troops, officered by the British. There was little artillery, and only 32 aircraft. When General Iida's 15th Army attacked with two under-strength divisions on 19 January 1942, Japanese aircraft, operating from airfields captured in December, had already inflicted heavy damage on the capital Rangoon and other military targets. Resistance was limited and when the Indian 17th Division, defending Rangoon, was isolated on the wrong side of the Sittang River after the bridge was blown up prematurely, the Allied front collapsed. Some 3,300 Indian soldiers succeeded in crossing the river, but all their equipment was abandoned. The British 7th Armoured Brigade, newly arrived at the port, had to disembark and move almost at once into combat. Further reinforcement proved impossible and over the following two weeks Japanese forces converged on Rangoon from the north and captured the city on 8 March.

British Empire forces were fortunate not to suffer a similar fate to the defenders of Malaya. Extricating themselves from almost certain Japanese encirclement before Rangoon was captured, the Burma Corps, created on 19 March and placed under the command of Lieutenant General Slim, retreated in fighting order much of the length of the Irrawaddy river valley running through central Burma, reaching the Indian town of Imphal in late May after a hazardous trek through jungle, plain and mountain. Japanese forces, supported by units of the Thai army and members of the Burma Independence Army, moved rapidly east and north, cutting off communications with the Chinese army, whose 38th Division fought alongside Burmese and Indian troops in an effort to keep the Japanese away from the north of the country. On 25 April, the decision was taken

OPPOSITE: Japanese tanks and infantry cross a bridge somewhere in Burma in June 1942 after completing the defeat of British Empire and Chinese forces. The Japanese tanks were poorly armed and armoured compared with European tanks, but there were no Allied tanks to defend Burma in 1942.

RIGHT: British Commonwealth troops face the Japanese in a hastily dug trench on a river in Burma during the Japanese invasion. Most of the forces under British command were Burmese or Indian.

Dear friend,

I am an Allied fighter, I did not come here to do any harm to you who are my friends, I only want to do harm to the Japanese and chase them away from your country as quickly as possible. If you will lead me to the nearest Allied Military Post, my Government will give you a good reward.

LEFT: A "bloodchit" issued to Allied airmen flying over the Chindit Hills and Burma, designed to procure them safe passage in the event of capture if their aircraft was forced down. The airlift over the "Hump", as it was called, ferried supplies to Chinese nationalist armies fighting the Japanese.

BELOW: Indian army troops and vehicles outside the Burmese town of Pyinmana, which was bombed by Japanese aircraft in an incendiary attack in April 1942, shortly before the British decision to abandon Burma.

OPPOSITE: A Chinese soldier in camouflage runs through the Burmese jungle during the campaign against the Japanese in 1942. The Chinese army sent units to help the British because it was essential to keep open the Burma Road supply route.

by the British authorities to abandon Burma, and Chinese forces in the north retreated back into Yunnan province. The Japanese army reached the Chinese border by 17 June and captured the airfield at Akyab, on the Bay of Bengal, on 4 May. Over the following months, Japan consolidated control of the region but, with British Empire forces entrenched at Imphal, and after a gruelling six-month campaign, no effort was made to push on further into India.

The Japanese occupiers allowed the Burma Independence Army to rule parts of the country after the expulsion of the British, and Burma was nominally granted "independence" in August 1943, when the Burmese premier, Ba Maw, declared war on the Allies, the last state to do so. Japan nevertheless controlled the economy of the region and in reality acted as an occupying power with a significant garrison to guard the outer reaches of the new Japanese empire.

FIELD MARSHAL WILLIAM SLIM (1891–1970)

Most of Field Marshal William Slim's soldiering was conducted in India and the Middle East following service at Gallipoli (where he was severely wounded) during the First World War. A brigadier in the Indian Army by 1939, he commanded an Indian army brigade in the conquest of Italian East Africa and then led the Indian 10th Division in the capture of Syria in June 1941. His powerful presence and popularity with his troops led to his appointment in March 1942 as commander of the Burmese Corps to try to stem the tide of Japanese advance through Burma. He orchestrated a successful retreat and later, in command of the 14th Army, he drove the Japanese back again across Burma in 1944. He was made a full general in 1945 and field marshal in 1949 while serving as Chief of the Imperial General Staff. He later served as Governor of Australia from 1953 to 1960, and ended his career as Governor of Windsor Castle.

30 MAY 1942

THE FIRST THOUSAND-BOMBER RAID

The bombing of German cities began in May 1940 and continued, when weather permitted and the forces were available, through to almost the last days of the war.

The early attacks were made with low performance twin-engined bombers with small bomb loads flying at night, many of which found it difficult to locate even the town they were supposed to attack. The arrival of the Vickers Wellington medium bomber in larger numbers in 1941 and 1942 made it possible to mount more significant raids, but the problem of scale and accuracy persisted. When Arthur Harris was appointed as Commander-in-Chief Bomber Command in February 1942, support for the bombing campaign was growing thin. A report based on investigation of photo-reconnaissance in the autumn of 1941, known as the Butt report after the civil servant who drew it up, showed that

only 20 per cent of aircraft actually attacked the 195 square kilometres (75 square miles) surrounding a designated target.

Harris set out to reinvigorate the bombing campaign and to show the politicians in Britain and the United States that bombing was a worthwhile strategy. His campaign was based on a directive issued by the Air Ministry on 14 February, before he took command, which detailed a list of German industrial cities as targets for what came to be known as "area bombing". Harris searched for an operation that would attract maximum publicity and in May decided on mounting a "thousand-bomber raid" against the western German city of Cologne. The operation was to bring together all available bomber aircraft, including those from the training schools, since there were only 400 operational bombers in frontline units. Instead of a cluster of bombers, Harris planned to use a bomber stream (in which all bombers flew at a single speed on a common route to the target, so overwhelming the defences), which was made possible by the introduction of a new navigation device, first used in a minor attack against Cologne on 13 March, known as Gee (Ground electronics engineering). Leading aircraft guided by the radio beam dropped flares and incendiaries to illuminate the target, while the bombers that followed dropped their bombs on the burning area one after the other. The result was a much larger concentration of more accurate bombing.

The attack was planned for 27 May but had to be postponed because of poor weather. Finally, after four days of waiting on alert, the crews were ordered to fly off on 30 May. The Gee-guided bombers found and illuminated the target and of the 1,050 aircraft assembled some 868 bombed the city. The attack resulted in the death of almost 500 people and the destruction of 12,000 dwellings, but did not seriously affect the industrial activity of the city. In all, 41 aircraft were lost to anti-aircraft fire and accident. Two days later, 956 bombers attacked the Ruhr city of Essen, and on 25 June 1,006 were assembled for an attack on the port of Bremen, but neither attack created serious levels of damage. In retaliation for earlier heavy raids on Lübeck and Rostock, the German air force launched the so-called Baedeker raids (an official in Berlin announced that British cities with three stars in the Baedeker tourist guide would be targeted) at the same time, killing 1,637 people in raids on Exeter, Norwich, Bath, York and Canterbury.

Harris achieved part of his purpose and bombing remained a central element in Britain's war effort, but the thousand-bomber raids were considered an extravagant use of scarce aircraft and more modest operations were planned thereafter, with increased bomb-load made possible by the introduction of the heavy Avro Lancaster, Short Stirling and Handley-Page Halifax bombers during the course of 1941 and 1942. In 1942, however, Bomber Command, joined by the bombers of the US 8th Air Force, dropped only 2.7 per cent of the total weight of bombs dropped throughout the whole war in Europe.

OPPOSITE: RAF ground crew preparing to arm a Vickers Wellington bomber with a 4,000lb bomb on 27 May 1942 at the bomber base at Mildenhall, Suffolk. Poor weather postponed the planned attack on Cologne for four days but crews had to remain on standby.

ABOVE: The stark ruins of the city of Cologne at the end of the war in 1945. Although the city was badly hit during Operation "Millennium", most of the damage to it was sustained in more than 200 raids experienced between 1942 and 1945.

14–21 JUNE 1942

CRISIS IN EGYPT: GAZALA AND TOBRUK

The results of Operation "Crusader", which had pushed Axis forces back across the Western Desert to El Agheila by December 1941, were reversed almost as soon as they were achieved.

Rommel, helped by the arrival of substantial supplies and reinforcements across the short Mediterranean supply route, launched a surprise counter-attack on 21 January 1942 which drove the tired British Empire forces more than halfway back to Egypt. The front stabilized at Gazala, where a line of strongpoints and minefields had been constructed stretching across the desert to the Free French garrison at Bir Hakeim. Neither side was in a position to take the initiative after months of combat in difficult conditions, and so the front stood firm at Gazala as both sides brought in reinforcements and fresh supplies of fuel and ammunition.

On 26 May, Rommel launched a renewed offensive. He had 560 tanks, almost half of them Italian, against a British Empire force of 700, recently reinforced with US-built Grant tanks. The Italian 10th and 21st Army Corps attacked the Allied front at Gazala in the north, while the bulk of Rommel's armoured forces swung south towards Bir Hakeim to try to encircle Ritchie's 8th Army. Although neither attack worked as Rommel had planned, the battle that followed showed how effective German armour could be in the hands of an imaginative commander. In the north, the Italian assault was held, while at Bir Hakeim, Free French forces offered stubborn resistance. Rommel was forced by 28 May to withdraw his forces, two German and two Italian armoured divisions, back into a defensive circle or "cauldron" (Kessel). Here he cleared minefields and with the help of "tank-busting" 88-milimetre (3.5-inch) anti-aircraft guns, repelled poorly co-ordinated attacks by British Empire forces from a zone codenamed "Knightsbridge" to the east of the "cauldron". By 1 June, Rommel was in a position to strike east in force and the Allied front crumbled. By 12 June, German armour and the Italian *Ariete* Division drove the enemy from Knightsbridge, while the Trieste Division was sent to help clear the French from Bir Hakeim, which finally succumbed on 10 June.

Unable to plug the gaps in the line, Ritchie ordered a retreat towards Tobruk, which was garrisoned by 35,000 troops, most of them South Africans. The 8th Army was unable to defend the port as it retreated in some disorder towards the Egyptian frontier, pursued by Rommel's armour. Tobruk was once again besieged but this time the defence was poorly organized and by 21 June, after an assault of only three days, the fortress was taken and with it 32,000 British Empire forces and their equipment and – from Rommel's point of view – vital supplies of fuel. The overall commander of British Empire forces in the Middle East, General Auchinleck, sacked Ritchie and took command himself. In order to avert complete disaster, which might have meant Axis control of the Suez Canal and access to the oil of the Middle East, Auchinleck abandoned the next defensive line further along the coast at Mersa Matruh, which was briefly contested between 27 and 29 June, for a more secure front at El Alamein and Alam Halfa, only 240 kilometres (150 miles) from Cairo. Though the scale was not the same as the struggle on the Russian steppe towards Stalingrad, there was a sense at Allied headquarters that the struggle for North Africa had reached its most critical stage. Axis armies here and in the Soviet Union seemed poised for victories that might turn the tide of war.

As Rommel's forces fast approached, the mood in Cairo worsened. Relations between the Egyptian population and the British Empire occupiers became increasingly strained, with food shortages and the sometimes disorderly behaviour of white troops. In February 1942, the British Resident Minister in Cairo had surrounded the royal palace with tanks and forced King Farouk to appoint a pro-British regime led by the Wafd Party. The King complied, but there remained important elements in the Egyptian military and political elite that waited expectantly for an Axis victory.

OPPOSITE: German tanks in desert camouflage make their way on 1 May 1942 towards the jumping-off point for the Axis attack launched against the British 8th Army on 26 May.

ABOVE: British POWs after the fall of Tobruk on 21 June walk past a German tank. The city fell after only a few days, having survived a prolonged siege during 1941.

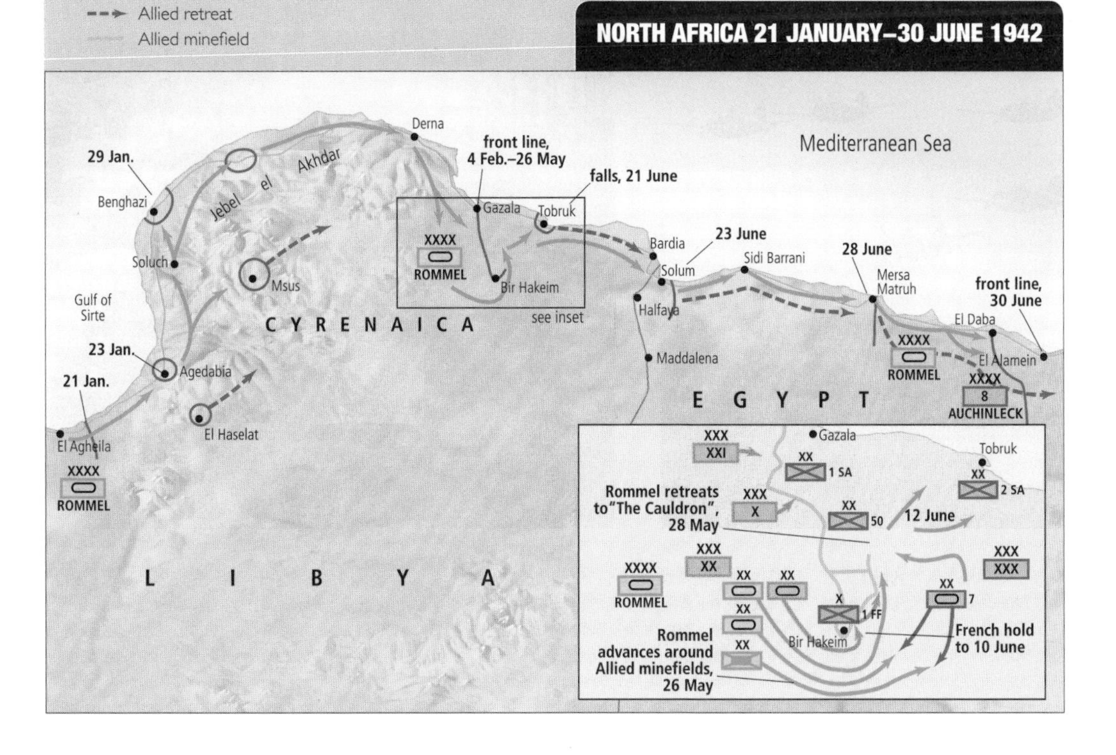

JANUARY 1942–MARCH 1943

THE BATTLE OF THE ATLANTIC

On 6 March 1941, stung by the high losses of merchant ships to German submarines during the winter months, Winston Churchill announced that Britain was now fighting "the Battle of the Atlantic".

The situation for the country was critical because so much of the raw material, oil and food the British war effort relied on, as well as the American aid promised through Lend Lease, had to be shipped across the Atlantic to British ports. In 1938, Britain imported 68 million tons of supplies, but in 1941 only 26 million. German submarines sank 1,299 ships in 1941 and the losses could not all be made good. By the spring of 1942, German naval commanders were convinced that Britain could be strangled into submission. So began a duel of the Royal Navy and the RAF against a force of around 300 German submarines under the command of Admiral Karl Dönitz, whose outcome was, as Churchill recognized, vital to the continued conduct of the war.

In the early months of 1942, following the entry of the United States into the war, German submarines, organized in packs with predatory codenames ("Leopard", "Panther" and "Puma") were sent to intercept American shipping. Unprepared for war, American ships were poorly equipped for anti-submarine warfare and could still be found sailing singly rather than in regular convoy. In the first four months of the year, 1.2 million tons of shipping was sunk off the American coast alone. Submarine losses were small, three in January, only two in February. The situation worsened over the year because the German B-Dienst intelligence unit had broken the British Naval Ciphers 2 and 3, directing convoy traffic across the Atlantic, while the British lost the knowledge they had gained from ULTRA when the German navy introduced the new Triton cipher in February. The Allies extended air patrols, forcing submarines into the so-called "Atlantic Gap" in mid-ocean, which aircraft could not reach,

OPPOSITE: The aerial view of an Atlantic convoy taken in May 1942. Thanks to careful intelligence work, well over half of all convoys crossed the ocean without loss. Submarines preyed particularly on stragglers and slower ships.

RIGHT: A flotilla of German submarines in port on the Atlantic coast of France. Over the course of the war around 1,000 German submarines were commissioned for the campaign against Allied merchant shipping.

BELOW: A German submarine under attack on the surface in June 1943 by aircraft from the USS *Bogue*. By the summer of 1943 most German submarines had been withdrawn to avoid catastrophic levels of loss.

but here the submarines preyed on weakly escorted convoys or convoy stragglers. During 1942, 7 million tons of shipping was lost in all areas, and by January 1943 the Royal Navy was down to just two months' supply of fuel.

The situation might well have deteriorated further without the work of the British Admiralty's Tracking Room and Trade Plot Room, both located in London, which used a variety of intelligence sources to assess the submarine threat and to route convoys safely. In the year between May 1942 and May 1943, 105 out of 174 convoys sailed without loss. During 1942, the Allies introduced new technology and tactics to try to blunt the submarine threat. Better explosive charges, improved Air-to-Surface-Vessel (ASV) radar and the introduction of powerful searchlights, known as "Leigh lights" after their inventor, all increased the kill chances against submarines. The accumulation of anti-submarine experience led to a sharp increase in sinkings during 1942 and forced the German submarines to operate in defined ocean areas.

In November 1942, with the appointment of Admiral Max Horton as Commander-in-Chief of the Western Approaches, which covered the main area of the submarine battle, greater efforts were devoted to organizing well-trained and powerful escort groups to hunt out the submarines rather than simply protect the convoys. But in the absence of detailed intelligence, and without aircraft cover, it proved difficult to reform the battle quickly. During February and March 1943, in exceptionally poor weather, the submarine war reached a crescendo with the sinking of 21 ships in mid-Atlantic for the loss of just one submarine. Over the following few weeks, the battle suddenly turned abruptly in favour of the Allies. New escort carriers and Very Long Range Liberator aircraft were introduced to bridge the "Gap"; the Triton cipher was finally broken; and all aircraft were fitted with the new ASV Mark III radar and Leigh lights. In April, 19 submarines were sunk, in May a further 41. German forces had no answer to the technical improvements, and on 24 May, Dönitz ordered submarines to retreat to their European bases, from which they continued to be attacked every time they ventured out to sea. In June 1943, not a single ship was lost in convoy and not a single attack reported. Although the submarine was not eliminated, the Battle of the Atlantic was effectively over.

19 AUGUST 1942

THE DIEPPE RAID

When Lord Louis Mountbatten became Chief of Combined Operations in March 1942, he inherited plans for small-scale raids on German-held coastlines to test their defences and secure intelligence.

Working together with the headquarters of the Home Army, Mountbatten and the Commanding Officer, South Eastern Command, Lieutenant General Bernard Montgomery, planned Operation "Rutter", a raid on the French port of Dieppe on the Channel coast. The raid was assigned to the Canadian 2nd Division, which was stationed in southern Britain, under the command of Major General John Roberts, and was to take place in July.

The purposes of the raid were not only operational. In the summer of 1942, there was strong pressure on the British War Cabinet from Moscow and Washington to show that Britain was capable of taking action against the German enemy. It was clear that no major cross-Channel invasion was possible in 1942 because of shortages of shipping and trained men, but the two men chosen to organize the raid, Mountbatten and the commander of No. 11 Group Fighter Command, Air Marshal Leigh-Mallory, were both strongly in favour of taking action against the enemy whenever possible. Leigh-Mallory had already organized what were called "Circuses", large groups of fighters with a few bombers to attack the north European coast and lure the German air force into battle. Mountbatten had already overseen the raids on St Nazaire and Bruneval.

Operation "Rutter" was on a different scale, but when the time for the assault came the weather caused its cancellation and Montgomery assumed that the plan was finished. Mountbatten revived it under a new codename, Operation "Jubilee". He kept the operation and its planning secret even from those under his command and it remains an open question whether the raid was ever formally approved by the Chiefs of Staff or the War Cabinet. The raid involved a total of 237 ships and landing craft, the Canadian Division, No. 3 and No. 4 Commandos, Royal Marine A Commando, 50 US Rangers and a total of 74 squadrons of aircraft, most of them

LEFT: A landing craft approaching the French shore during the Dieppe Raid of 19 August 1942 under cover of a smokescreen laid by RAF aircraft. The raid proved a disastrous gamble and alerted the Allies to the need for thorough preparation before a full-scale invasion.

OPPOSITE, MAIN: German soldiers inspect a destroyed British landing craft used during the raid on Dieppe. In all some 33 landing craft and one destroyer were lost during the operation out of a total of 237 ships of all kinds used for the raid.

OPPOSITE, INSET: No. 4 Special Service division shoulder title.

fighters. This considerable force crossed the Channel on 19 August. Intelligence information was poor and the assault plan – for a frontal attack on the port – carried dangerous risks. Two flank attacks on the guns on either side of Dieppe were made by the Commando units, but the one to the east was detected by a German convoy and the coastal garrison alerted. Only the batteries to the west were captured by No. 4 Commando. Half an hour after the flank attacks, at 5.20 in the morning, the main force landed on the port beaches under cover of a smokescreen. They came under heavy fire, and losses were high. Roberts called in his reserve forces to try to strengthen the assault, but the decision only compounded what was an evident disaster. The few tanks which were successfully landed either failed to scale the sea wall or were quickly immobilized in the town. By 11.00 a.m., the troops were ordered to withdraw and the evacuation of what was left of the force was completed by early afternoon.

The losses from the raid were exceptionally high. Out of the 4,963 Canadians, 3,367 were killed, wounded or captured. The total killed from all the forces committed was 1,027. The RAF lost 106 aircraft and destroyed only 48. The outcome had many causes, but the principal failure was not to recognize how difficult a frontal assault on a heavily defended port and coastline could be without prior bombing or naval gunfire, and with poor reconnaissance preparation. The lessons of Dieppe were absorbed in the later preparations for the landings in France, but the immediate impact was to rule out any prospect in the near future of a "Second Front" to help the Soviet war effort.

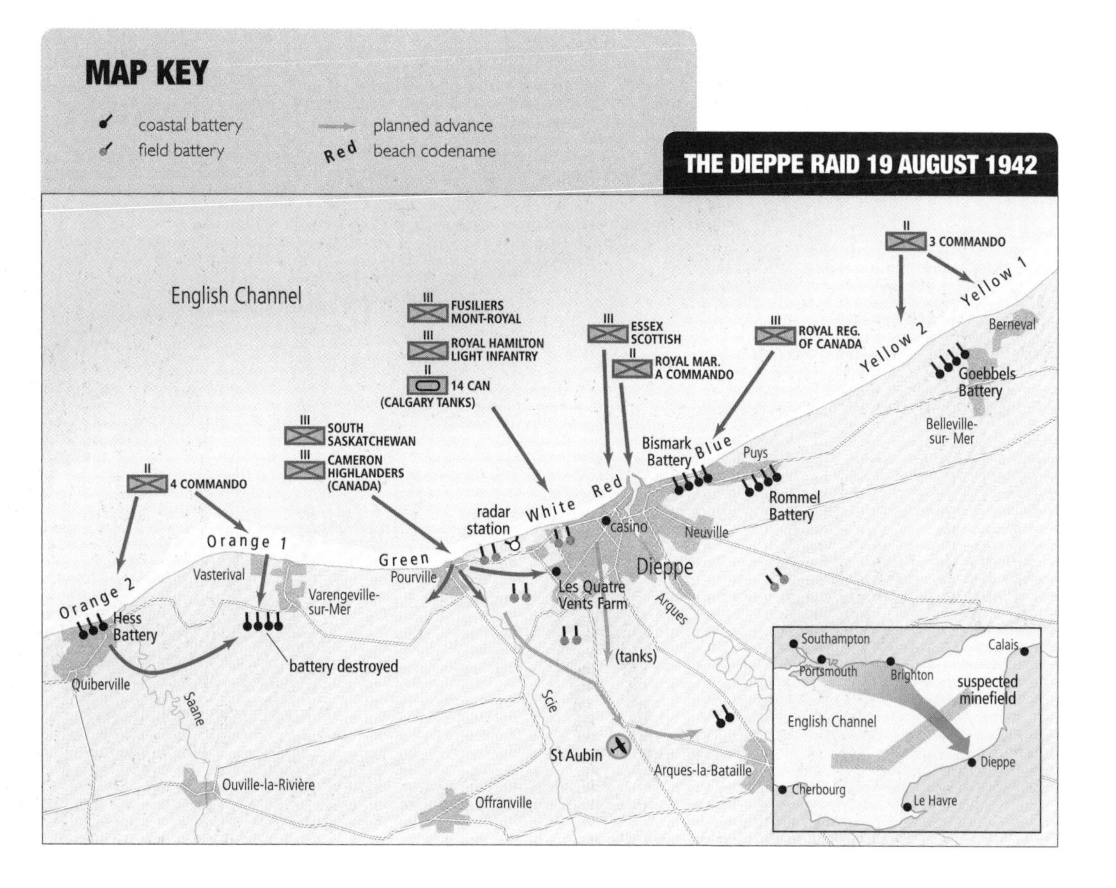

30 AUGUST–7 SEPTEMBER 1942

THE TIDE TURNS IN NORTH AFRICA

When Rommel's successful Axis offensive reached into Egypt to the Alamein Line in June 1942, he was determined to push on to capture Cairo and the Suez Canal.

His success in the summer offensive had earned him the rank of field marshal. On 1 July, the Axis forces attacked the Allied defensive line but British Commonwealth forces were dug in well and the attacks were repulsed. General Auchinleck then decided on a counter-offensive, taking advantage of a substantial superiority in tanks and aircraft. The attacks, launched on 10 July, proved a costly failure. Rommel was prevented from going any further, but Allied tank strength, which had been four times that of Rommel's forces, was severely

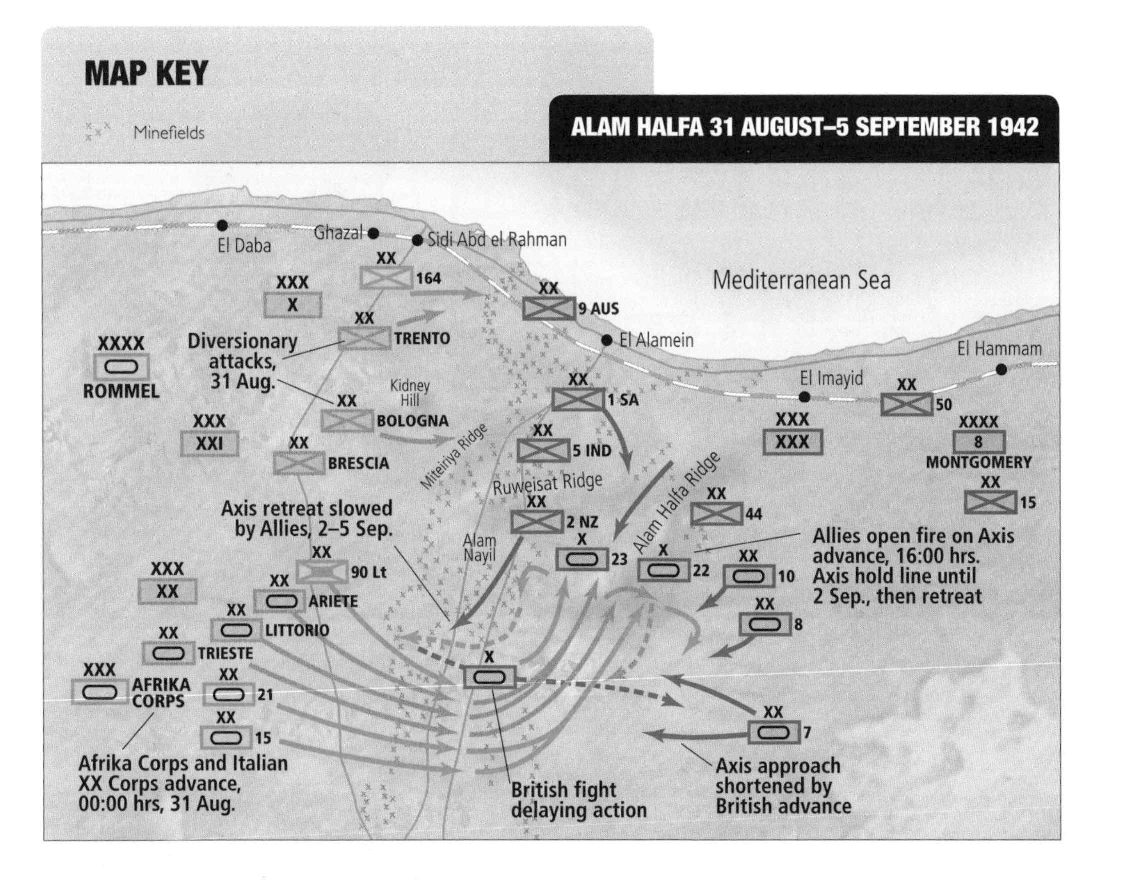

reduced. Allied casualties from what became known as the First Battle of El Alamein were over 13,000.

Churchill, frustrated at repeated failure, removed Auchinleck and replaced him as commander-in-chief Middle East with General Harold Alexander. Command of the 8th Army was given to Lieutenant General William Gott, but he died on 7 August, when the transport plane in which he was travelling was shot down. His replacement, Lieutenant General Bernard Montgomery, was to forge a remarkable alliance with Alexander which led Allied armies across North Africa and on into Sicily and Italy. Montgomery was reluctant to commit to a further offensive until he had substantial additional forces; instead the defensive line was strengthened in anticipation of a further German assault, whose details had been revealed by ULTRA decrypts.

Rommel's plan was to mount a diversionary attack towards the Australian and South African forces on the coast around El Alamein, while taking the bulk of his armour and that of his Italian ally in a wide southern sweep to outflank the Allied line and encircle Montgomery's forces. It was an ambitious but predictable move and Montgomery prepared his forces to meet the encircling Axis on the high ridge at Alam Halfa, some 25 kilometres (15 miles) behind Allied lines. Short of fuel and with a limited number of tanks,

OPPOSITE: Italian Fascism continued to pretend that Italy was a powerful military state despite defeats in Africa. Here a wartime military parade in front of visiting German dignitaries in the Piazza Venezia in Rome is supposed to display the might of the new Italy.

BELOW: Armband awarded to German forces who took part in the North Africa campaigns.

FIELD MARSHAL HAROLD ALEXANDER (1891–1969)

Harold Alexander was one of Britain's most successful wartime commanders. After a distinguished combat career in the First World War, he became the youngest general in the army in 1937. He commanded the First Division in France in 1940 and then commanded the BEF (British Expeditionary Force) during the Dunkirk evacuation. In March 1942 he organized the British retreat from Burma, and was appointed commander-in-chief Middle East in August 1942. In early 1943 he became Eisenhower's deputy for the campaign in Tunisia, where he reorganized a poorly co-ordinated Allied front and forced Axis surrender in May. He commanded the invasion of Sicily and Italy and in November 1944 was made supreme commander in the Mediterranean. Created a field marshal in September 1944, he was governor general of Canada from 1946 to 1952.

Rommel began the attack on the night of 30/31 August with four armoured units, the German 15th and 21st Panzer, and the Italian Ariete and Littorio divisions. They made rapid progress through the series of defensive "boxes" on the south of the Allied line and turned on Alam Halfa ridge to complete the encirclement.

Montgomery's strategy worked just as intended. Axis forces became bogged down in extensive minefields, were attacked on the flank by the British 7th Armoured Division and hit by effective anti-tank fire from forces dug in on the ridge. After two days of fruitless fighting, Rommel ordered a retreat, leaving 50 tanks and 400 vehicles behind. This was the furthest Axis forces got in the North African campaign, and the last prospect that Rommel had of snatching a rapid victory. Over the next two months Rommel established a thick defensive line against the expected counter-offensive, with wide minefields and armoured divisions dug in behind them.

The victory at Alam Halfa has attracted none of the attention given to the eventual victory at Alamein in November, but it was an important turning point and it gave Montgomery the opportunity to display his mettle while Churchill pressed him for action. It was a victory won by substantial superiority in weapons and supplies. The Middle Eastern air force comprised 96 squadrons of more than 1,000 aircraft by October 1942, with a genuinely international flavour. Beside units staffed by British crew, there were American, South African, Australian, Greek, Canadian, French, Rhodesian and Yugoslav squadrons. Air power proved a substantial bonus for Allied forces as the German and Italian air component dwindled, hampered by regular shortages of fuel oil. These advantages were to prove decisive in the next, and most famous, of Montgomery's offensives.

ABOVE: A German soldier uses a "donkey's ears" periscope to observe Allied lines during the probing attacks organized by Rommel in early July 1942.

LEFT: British forces depended on generous supplies from the United States for the Middle Eastern campaigns. Here the 5th Royal Tank Regiment displays its Grant tanks for the camera on 17 February 1942.

BELOW: Churchill flew to Cairo in August 1942 to see for himself what should be done to ensure that North Africa could be defended. Here he sits with the South African premier Jan Smuts with, behind, General Alan Brooke (right) and Air Marshal Arthur Tedder (left).

BOTTOM: Supply was a big advantage the Allies held over the Axis in North Africa because Axis supply routes were easily interrupted by Allied submarine and air attack. Here a convoy unloads RAF parts and equipment in Port Said in Egypt in August 1942.

23 OCTOBER–4 NOVEMBER 1942

SECOND ALAMEIN

The Second Battle of El Alamein was the first major victory of British Commonwealth forces against the German enemy and it opened the way to the destruction of Axis forces throughout North Africa.

Although the battle was dwarfed by the campaigns on the Eastern Front, it was nonetheless a decisive turning point in Allied fortunes, making the Middle East secure and opening the way for a campaign to liberate the Mediterranean from the Axis.

Rommel knew after the failure at Alam Halfa that he lacked the depth of resources needed to penetrate further into Egypt. Instead, he established a thick defensive line, providing German troops and tanks to strengthen the Italian divisions; the greatest concentration of Axis forces was in the north, protecting communications along the coast. Rommel had four German and a maximum of eight Italian divisions at his disposal (a balance reflected in the decision to rename Panzer Army Africa the German-Italian Panzer Army). The Axis fielded around 500 tanks, of which fewer than half were German, and had support from 350 aircraft. All Axis forces were short of fuel and spare parts. Montgomery, on the other hand, saw his forces grow steadily during September and October. The armoured divisions could call on 1,030 tanks, 300 of which were new American Grants, and there were over 1,500 aircraft in the Middle East and Malta. He refused to act until he was confident that his forces had a decisive superiority and the army understood the nature of his plan.

After years of rapid mobile warfare, the Second Alamein battle was a set-piece operation. Montgomery planned to attack where Rommel was strongest in the north, around Kidney Hill, but to disguise the weight of his assault by diversionary attacks in the south. His object, in what was codenamed Operation "Lightfoot", was to send forward the infantry divisions to open up a pathway through the minefields, and then to pour the tanks of the 10th Armoured Corps through the gap. With a salient secured, a second operation, "Supercharge", would push through large armoured forces for the final blow. The start was set for 23 October, when fortuitously Rommel was away on sick leave.

Operation "Lightfoot" began with a massive artillery barrage in the evening of 23 October. Rommel's replacement, Lieutenant General Stumme, died during the Allied air

ABOVE LEFT: Formation badge for the British 7th Armoured Division, known as the "Desert Rats".

ABOVE RIGHT: Badge of the 51st Highland Infantry Division.

OPPOSITE: British infantry advance through the dust and smoke of combat during the Second Battle of Alamein, October 1942.

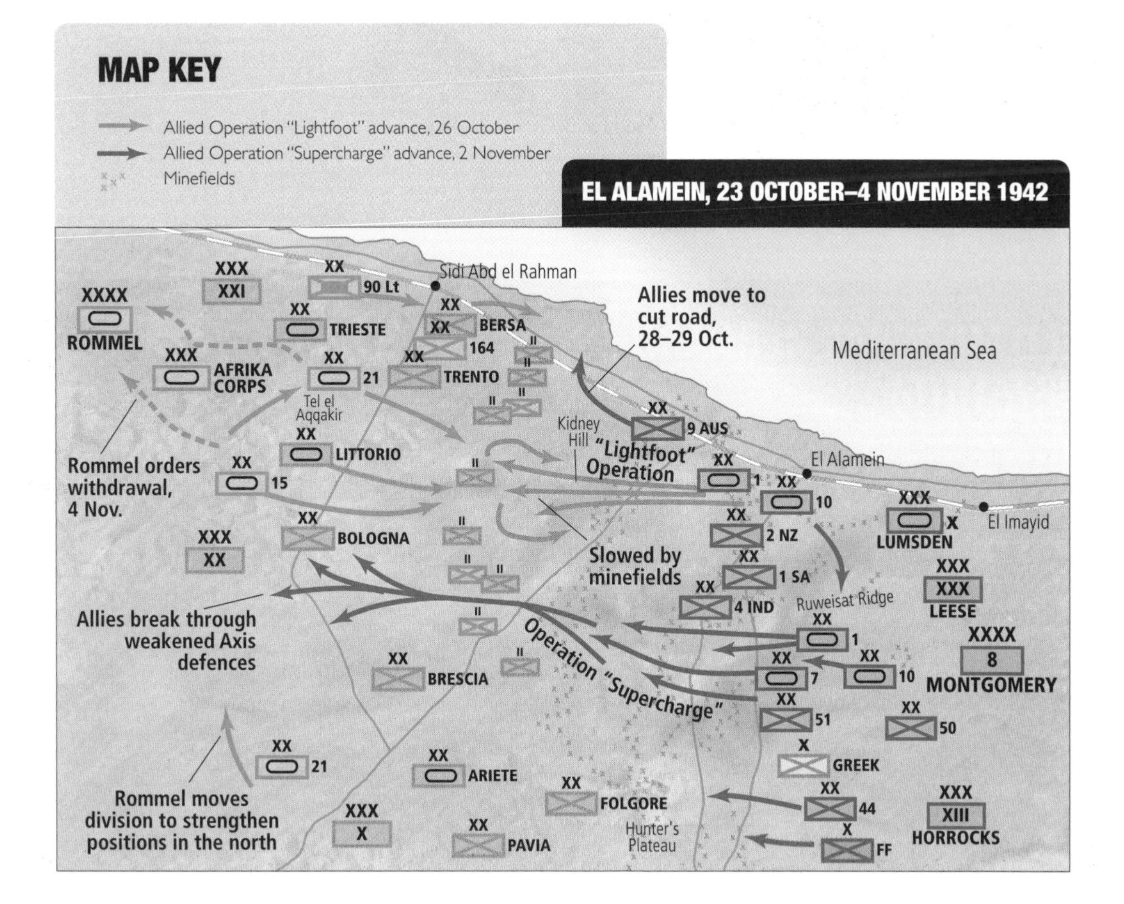

attacks, leaving Axis forces in some confusion until Rommel's return on 25 October. Nevertheless, resistance was fierce, and only by the second day was progress made along the coast road and around Kidney Hill. Rommel ordered his tanks north to dislodge the enemy, but exposed the Italian divisions to Allied attacks, which were pressed forward during fierce armoured fighting on 27 and 28 October. Montgomery then withdrew the diversionary forces in the south and concentrated a heavy armoured force to carry out "Supercharge". When the fresh armour poured through on 2 November, supported by strong air attacks, Rommel realized he was defeated; Axis forces were down to only 35 fully serviceable tanks. Hitler refused permission to withdraw, but two days later he had to accept reality, and Rommel began a rapid westwards retreat along the coast road. Some Italian divisions continued to fight after the German forces had abandoned the battle, but the Axis position was hopeless. Rommel left over 400 destroyed tanks; the Allies lost around 250. Allied casualties were 13,500, but Montgomery's forces netted over 30,000 Axis prisoners.

The 8th Army raced in pursuit of the retreating Rommel and by 13 November had retaken Tobruk. Axis forces made brief defensive attacks at Benghazi on 20 November and El Agheila between 23 November and 13 December, but the pressure was relentless. Tripoli was occupied on 23 January and Rommel raced for the last defensive line in Tunisia, the Mareth Line, where Axis forces finally halted and turned. Victory at Alamein was complete and permission was given for church bells in Britain to ring out in celebration for the first time since May 1940.

LEFT: German soldiers man the tank-busting 88-millimetre (3.5-inch) anti-aircraft gun during the Battle of Alamein. It was found that the gun could be used against tanks as well as aircraft and was very effective against Allied tanks throughout the war.

FIELD MARSHAL BERNARD MONTGOMERY (1887–1976)

The son of an Anglo-Irish clergyman, Montgomery joined the army in 1908 and saw service in the early battles of the First World War before a bullet in the lung almost killed him. He returned to duty as a staff officer, and served between the wars in Ireland, India, Egypt and Palestine, where he was responsible for suppressing a revolt in 1938. He made his reputation as an excellent trainer of men and a master of meticulous preparation. In the Battle of France he commanded the 3rd Division, which he successfully withdrew at Dunkirk with relatively low casualties. In December 1941 he was appointed commander-in-chief Southeastern Command, where he insisted on intensive training for his men. Appointed to command the 8th Army in August 1942, he transformed its morale in a matter of weeks. El Alamein was his most famous victory, and subsequent campaigns in Sicily, Italy and northwest Europe made him a household name. He was a difficult personality – acerbic, intolerant, boastful, egotistical – and this soured his strategic performance. He collaborated poorly with others; tact was entirely foreign to him. He was ground commander for the Normandy invasion, then commander of the 21st Army Group. After the war, he was appointed chief of the Imperial General Staff and created Viscount Montgomery of Alamein.

ABOVE: A British Bofors mobile anti-aircraft gun being moved forward in November 1942 to the Libyan frontier, past a dead German soldier, left unburied during the rapid Axis retreat.

RIGHT A British Daimler-Benz armoured car opens fire at the start of the attack on German-held Tripoli, 18 January 1943. The port fell to the Allies five days later.

BELOW: Sherman tanks of the Allied armoured forces in North Africa move swiftly along desert routes in pursuit of the retreating German and Italian forces after the victory at El Alamein in November 1942.

Policy of Army Commander BGS Most Secret
issued at 0900 hrs 26 October Appx

1. 51 DIV. area must be tidied up, and there must be no enemy left inside it.

2. 10 Corps are relieved by Army Comd of any responsibility for the security of bridgehead area in order to concentrate 100 per cent on its own task. Task of 10 Corps is to make progress to the west and north-west from the Kidney Hill area.

3. Consequent on para 2, 30 Corps must ensure that bridgehead area is so re-organized and held that Divisions can withstand, unaided, attacks by armoured and unarmoured formations.

4. Operations of 30 Corps to be of a minor nature for the present, and to be conducted with a view to assisting 10 Corps to get clear and make progress west and north-west.

5. While 30 Corps are conducting only minor operations, vide para 4, Divisions of that corps to be so reorganized and rested that they can conduct major operations in the near future.

6. On the 13 Corps front, no further tank casualties are to be risked in 7 Armd DIV by using that Division offensively.

7. The weight of the available air power will be directed against the enemy army opposing Eighth Army. Air operations will be designed to assist our progress in the north.

Copies to: 10 Corps
13 Corps
30 Corps
A.O.C.

ABOVE: The orders of General Bernard Montgomery for the third day of the Second Battle of Alamein, 26 October 1942, codenamed Operation "Lightfoot". Fierce German counter-attacks were met by regrouping British Commonwealth forces. A week later the Axis line was broken and Rommel in retreat.

[BLM 1/77]

Address to Officers – "Lightfoot". 19/20 Oct 1942

1. Back history since August. The Mandate; my plans to carry it out; the creation of 10 Corps. Leadership – equipment – training.

2. Interference by Rommell on 31 Aug.

3. The basis framework of the Army plan for Lightfoot as issued on 14 Sep. To destroy enemy armour.

4. Situation in early October. Untrained Army. Gradually realized that ~~I~~ must recast the plan so as to be within the capabilities of the troops. The new plan; the "crumbling" operations. A reversal of accepted methods.

5 Key points in the Army plan. Three phases.

30 Corps break-in.
10 Corps break through. } Fighting for position and
13 Corps break in. } the tactical advantage.

The dog-fight, and "crumbling" operations.

The final "break" of the enemy.

6. The enemy.

His sickness; low strengths; small stocks of petrol, ammunition, food.
Morale is good, except possibly Italians.

7. Ourselves.

Immense superiority in guns, tanks, men.
Can fight a prolonged battle, & will do so

25 pdr 832
6 pdr 753
2 pdr 500

1200 tanks (470 heavy)

Morale on the top line.

8. General conduct of the battle.

Methodical progress; destroy enemy part by part, slowly and surely.
Shoot tanks and shoot Germans.
He cannot last a long battle; we can.
We must therefore keep at it hard; no unit commander must relax the pressure;
Organize ahead for a "dog fight" of a week. Whole affair about ~~10~~ days, (12).

Don't expect spectacular results too soon.
Operate from firm bases.
Quick re-organization on objectives.
Keep balanced.
Maintain offensive eagerness.
Keep up the pressure.

} If we do all victory certain

12. Morale – measures to get it. Addresses.
Every soldier in the Army a fighting soldier.
No non-fighting man. All trained to kill Germans.
My message to the troops.

11. The issues at stake.

10. The troops to remember what to say if they are captured. Rank, name, & number.

B.L.M.

8 FEBRUARY–30 APRIL 1943

OPERATION "LONGCLOTH": THE CHINDITS IN BURMA

When combat came to an end in Burma (Myanmar) in 1942, a stalemate followed.

The Japanese were too overstretched to attempt to penetrate any further, but British Indian forces in Assam needed to regroup, retrain and prepare thoroughly for warfare in the inhospitable conditions of Burma. An ill-prepared attack on the port of Akyab on the Burmese coast in autumn and winter 1942–43 ended in disaster, with no ground gained and 5,000 casualties.

The commander-in-chief in India, General Archibald Wavell, had invited Lieutenant Colonel Orde Wingate to India in March 1942 to prepare special forces for action behind Japanese lines. Wingate had served under Wavell in Palestine before the war and in East Africa in 1940–41. His force was officially designated the 77th Indian Infantry Brigade, but it was always known

by the nickname "Chindits", derived from the Burmese word *chinthé*, a mythical winged lion, whose carved image was common on temples in Burma. Wingate developed the idea of long-range penetration operations using small units of specially trained men to infiltrate Japanese-held territory, cutting vital communication links and harassing the enemy. Although Wavell approved the tactic in principle, he was reluctant to endorse the idea of a risky adventure, but Wingate finally persuaded him to allow an experimental operation. Codenamed "Longcloth", it was planned for February 1943.

The Chindit force was organized into seven columns, each with between 400 and 500 men. The plan was to supply them from the air so that they could move with little equipment, and independent of any supply line. On the night of 14/15 February 1943, they crossed the Chindwin River into Burma, those columns commanded by Wingate moving north, and two columns heading southeast towards the Irrawaddy river. They succeeded in crossing large areas of the country and destroyed railway lines and bridges, but they also encountered Japanese forces, fighting at least nine engagements. Air supply was difficult to organize, and the Chindits found themselves short of food and supplies and crippled by disease. Instead of moving to the planned area of operation for the period up to May around the town of Pago, they were ordered to make their way back to India in late March.

OPPOSITE: Chindit soldiers with mules trekking through the Burmese jungle. They had to carry with them everything they needed, but food was always scarce.

ABOVE: Major General Orde Wingate (centre, with hat) briefing men of the 77th Indian Infantry Brigade at an airfield at Sylhet in Assam before an operation. The forces that Wingate led into Burma had to be supplied entirely from the air.

Out of the original 3,000 men, some 818 were dead or prisoners-of-war, and many of the rest too ill to continue. The operation achieved little in strategic terms, but it did act to boost morale in the Indian army, by showing that Japanese troops were not invincible. Wingate also won Churchill's admiration and the small guerrilla force became temporary heroes. Wingate was invited to attend the Quebec Conference in August 1943, where generous funds and equipment were put at his disposal. The operation also prompted the Japanese military to accept the need for a pre-emptive campaign of their own, which they launched in March 1944 against the towns of Imphal and Kohima in Indian Assam.

A second Chindit operation, codenamed "Thursday", was organized in February 1944 with some 20,000 special forces, designed to impede the Japanese assault on India. But Wingate's death in an air crash in March led to the abandonment of his irregular, deep-penetration tactics and the force fought in conventional formation alongside the forces of General Stilwell and elements of the Chinese army. This campaign also proved costly, with 3,628 casualties among the original Chindit force. The force was wound up in February 1945. Although their military achievements were modest, the Chindit campaigns were a model of heroism and endurance.

MAJOR GENERAL ORDE WINGATE (1903–44)

Orde Wingate was one of the most unorthodox officers in the British army. A regular officer who served in Palestine in the 1930s, where he became a Zionist, he joined SOE (Special Operations Executive) and in the East African campaign in early 1941 formed "Gideon Force", an irregular guerrilla unit which fought in Ethiopia with the exiled emperor, Haile Selassie. He was virtually dismissed for insubordination after the campaign, and attempted suicide. In 1942, he was summoned by General Wavell to India to organize guerrilla combat against the Japanese in Burma. His "Chindit" force fought in 1943 and again in 1944, but he was killed in an air crash on 24 March 1944 before the second campaign had got very far. He had a mixed reputation. Rude, opinionated and irreverent, he also inspired loyalty among his men and the strong support of Winston Churchill, who liked his unconventional view of warfare.

LEFT: Merrill's Marauders in action in the Pacific jungle, December 1943.

RIGHT: Formation badge of the 3rd Infantry Division – the Chindits.

OPPOSITE: Chindit forces prepare to blow a railway line far behind Japanese lines in Burma. They cut the main Mandalay–Lashio link before returning to India in March 1943.

MERRILL'S MARAUDERS

After the first Chindit campaign, an American force was raised to fight the Japanese in Burma using the same methods. The 3,000-strong force was codenamed "Galahad"; its official title was 5307 Composite Unit, but it was known as "Merrill's Marauders" after the group's commander, Brigadier General Frank Merrill. It trained with the Chindits, and was then assigned to work with the American General Joseph Stilwell and his Chinese forces in an operation against Japanese forces in northern Burma between February and August 1944. Despite early successes, the unit, like the Chindits in 1943, suffered from heavy losses, particularly due to disease and the arduous conditions in which they had to fight. In the end the force was decimated and at the end of the campaign was disbanded, its surviving members absorbed into the regular US army.

RIGHT: A Chindit column crossing a river somewhere in Burma. They were organized into small self-contained groups to operate behind the lines. They all marched at least 1,000 miles during Operation "Longcloth".

BELOW: Transport aircraft towing gliders fly towards Burma for a later Chindit operation in early 1944. The first wave of Chindits would be landed by glider and then prepare airfields for further aircraft to land.

14 FEBRUARY–13 MAY 1943

THE END OF THE AXIS IN AFRICA: TUNISIA

After the success of the Second Battle of Alamein and the "Torch" landings in North Africa, the Allies had hoped to complete the elimination of enemy resistance within weeks.

Instead Rommel successfully brought his battered Afrika Korps back to southern Tunisia by the end of January 1943, while in the north the 5th Panzer Army and the remnants of the Italian 1st Army, despite shortages of equipment, oil and ammunition, established a new Axis front line running the whole length of Tunisia.

The Allied plan was to try to divide the northern force under General von Arnim from Rommel's forces in the south with a drive by the US 1st Armored Division to the coastal port of Sfax (Operation "Satin"). But shortages of supply led to the cancellation of "Satin", and instead von Arnim and then Rommel took the initiative in attacking the US 2nd Corps from the eastern Dorsale Mountains in central Tunisia. On 14 February, the American force was driven back to the Kasserine Pass, and there, on 20 February Rommel, some of whose forces had moved up from the southern Mareth Line, inflicted a heavy defeat on the retreating American army. German units pushed on beyond the pass, but by 22 February they were halted by British and American counter-attacks. Rommel moved back through the mountains, and moved south to defend against an anticipated attack by Montgomery's 8th Army.

The baptism of fire for American forces against experienced German and Italian troops was a harsh one. Relations between the American, British and French forces were strained and supplies were difficult to bring across the long North African routes in poor weather and mud. Eisenhower appointed General Alexander to restore order to the Allied front and complete the destruction of the Axis pocket. Much depended on Montgomery breaching the Mareth Line, but in early March Rommel launched his own offensive. On 6 March, three Panzer divisions moved forward, but Montgomery, warned in advance by decrypted German messages, had prepared a trap. Rommel's tanks ran into a wall of withering anti-tank fire and were forced to retreat. On 9 March, Rommel flew to see Hitler to demand more assistance, but instead he was ordered on sick leave, his command taken by von Arnim.

LEFT: Local inhabitants in Tunis leave the city during the spring of 1943 to avoid the final showdown between Allied and Axis forces which reached its peak in May.

OPPOSITE: General von Arnim, the German commander in Tunisia after Rommel's departure to Germany on health grounds, shortly after the Axis surrender on 12 May 1943.

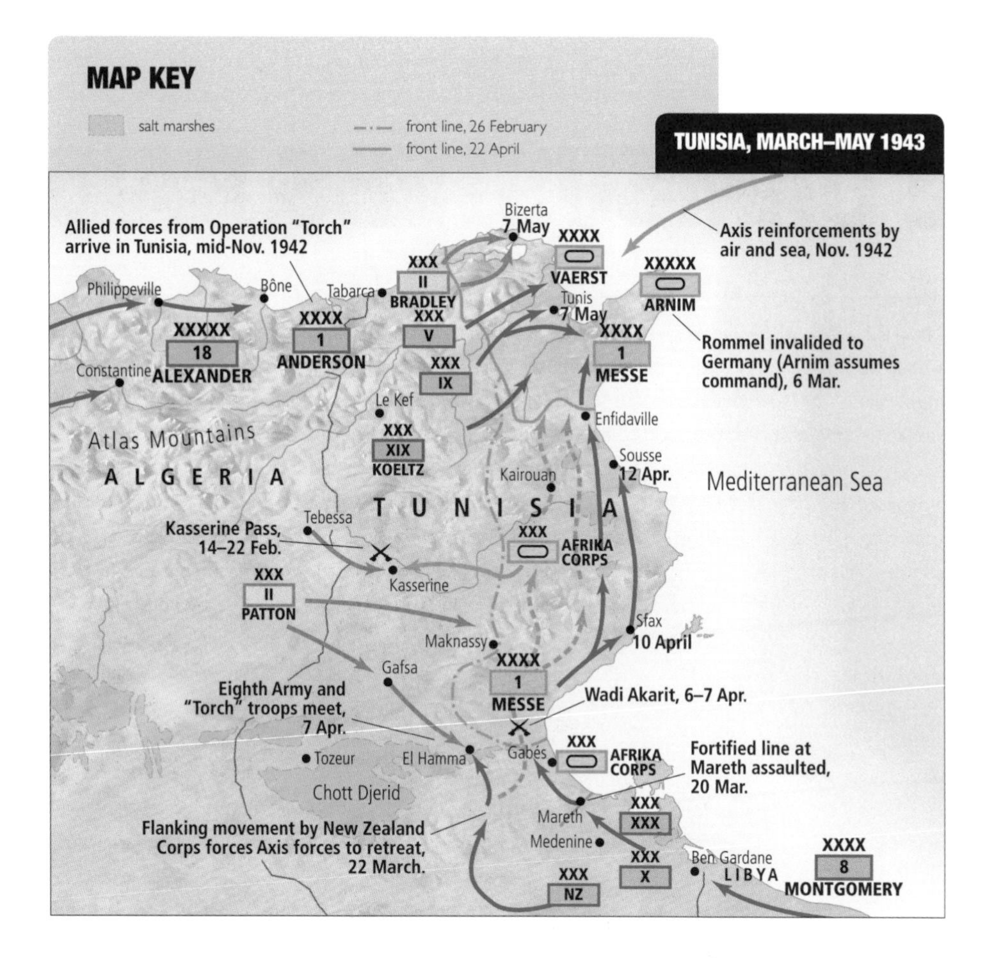

On 20–21 March, Montgomery attacked with the bulk of the 8th Army against the Mareth defences, while the New Zealand Division was sent in a wide outflanking movement through hilly country to capture El Hamma in the Axis rear. Poor weather made progress slow in the frontal assault, and further armour was sent on the flanking attack. To the north, Alexander ordered the US 2nd Corps to drive for the coast and cut off the Axis retreat. The assault proved too difficult, and when Axis forces were compelled in late March to abandon the Mareth Line, they moved northwards, pursued by the 8th Army until they met up with the remaining German and Italian forces in the north of the country. On 7 April, 8th Army troops met up with American forces coming from the northwest.

Von Arnim and the Italian commander, Marshal Messe, organized a final stand in the northeast corner of the country around Bizerta and Tunis. They judged their position to be hopeless, but after a meeting between Hitler and Mussolini in Salzburg on 8 April, they were ordered to hold fast at all costs. Supply was down to a fraction of what was needed. In three weeks in April, Allied fighter aircraft destroyed 432 Axis planes for the loss of just 35, including half the entire German air transport fleet. Axis forces had just 150 tanks, against more than 1,500 on the Allied side. Alexander ordered the American 2nd Corps to the north opposite the port of Bizerta; the British 1st Army under Lieutenant General Kenneth Anderson stood opposite Tunis; while the 8th Army occupied the southern section of the Allied noose. On 6 May, a general offensive was launched. Bombarded from the air and artillery, short of almost all essential supplies, Axis resistance collapsed. Bizerta and Tunis fell on 7 May, and five days later von Arnim, who had retreated to the very furthest tip of Tunisia on Cape Bon, surrendered. Marshal Messe, further south, surrendered to Montgomery a day later with the scattered remnants of his 1st Italian Army. Some 240,000 prisoners were taken, a defeat that ranked in numbers with Stalingrad three months before.

17 MAY 1943

THE DAMBUSTERS RAID

The decision to attack the major dams in the German Ruhr valley originated with the development of a "bouncing bomb" by the British engineer Barnes Wallis, who was convinced that attacking Germany's water supply would have a crippling effect on production and morale.

The drum-shaped bomb was designed to rotate at speed as it was dropped from no more than 28 metres (60 feet) and then bounce across the surface of the water until reaching the dam wall, when it would spin to the foot of the wall and explode. The bomb was extensively tested and found to be a viable design. There then followed efforts to persuade the Air Ministry that an operation against the dams would work.

In Bomber Command there was a prejudice against what the commander-in-chief Arthur Harris called "panacea targets". The strategy pursued during 1942 and 1943 was to attack major industrial cities in order to reduce German economic

OPPOSITE: An aerial reconnaissance photograph of the Möhne Dam taken before the Dambusters Raid. Together with the Sorpe Dam, the reservoirs supplied 75 per cent of the water needed by Ruhr industry.

RIGHT: The production of shells in a factory in the Ruhr industrial region in 1942. The attack on the dams was supposed to undermine armaments production but it had very little direct effect.

capability, rather than attack a particular industrial or utility target. Harris finally agreed and aircraft were released to form what was called at first "Squadron X", but became designated 617 Squadron. The plan to bomb the dams was accepted on 26 February 1943, and there followed an intensive period of training in low-altitude flying and the use of the bouncing bomb, codenamed "Upkeep". A special aiming device was developed to ensure that the bomb was released at the right moment, and spotlights placed in the nose and tail of the Lancaster bombers used for the raid to provide a guide to altitude. By early May, the preparations were complete.

The operation, codenamed "Chastise", was undertaken on the night of 16/17 May 1943. The attacking force was organized into

BARNES WALLIS (1887–1979)

A British aeronautical engineer, Barnes Wallis was responsible for developing a number of different aircraft and bomb designs during the Second World War. He joined the Vickers armaments company as a young engineer in 1913 and remained with the firm until his retirement in 1971. He designed the revolutionary geodesic airframe, first for airships, then in the Wellington bomber, an exceptionally sturdy aircraft capable of sustaining high levels of damage and still remaining airborne. He designed the bomb for the dams raid, and later the "Tallboy" and "Grand Slam" bombs for deep-penetration attacks. After 1945, he pioneered the "swing-wing" concept for fighter aircraft but saw his ideas developed first by American aircraft producers.

three groups: Formation 1 was to attack the Möhne Dam and, if there were bombs left, proceed to the Eder Dam; Formation 2 was to attack the Sorpe Dam; and a third reserve formation was to take off later and attack any dams that had not yet been breached. On the outward flight, the first formation lost one aircraft, while of the five aircraft in the second formation only one survived to reach the target: two were forced back and two were destroyed. The attack on the Möhne Dam was carried out successfully and the five surviving aircraft then flew to the Eder Dam, which was shrouded in fog. The final bombing run successfully breached the target. Formation 2 now consisted of one aircraft, whose bomb hit the Sorpe Dam but did not destroy it. Unlike the first two targets, the Sorpe was not made of concrete but of earth. Reserve aircraft then attacked but no further damage was caused.

The raid resulted in the loss of 11 bombers out of 19 and the loss of 53 out of 133 crewmen. The effect of the raids proved a disappointment to the planners. A huge area of flooding around 80 kilometres (50 miles) in length killed an estimated 1,650 people (including 1,026 POWs and foreign forced labourers) and inundated farmland. But Ruhr industry was hardly affected, electricity supplies were soon restored, and by 27 June there was a full water supply again. German authorities were alarmed by the prospect of a sustained attack against the Reich's water supply, but the operation was not repeated and Bomber Command returned to the strategy

LEFT: Wing Commander Guy Gibson and his crew board their Lancaster bomber for the attack on the dams, 17 May 1943. He was one of the lucky ones to return.

RIGHT: Albert Speer (left), the German minister for weapons and munitions, visiting the Möhne Dam after its destruction by RAF 617 Squadron. Emergency water supplies could be found within days of the attack and the dams were repaired rapidly thereafter.

of area bombing. Harris remained unconvinced of the value of attacking a single target-system, and was later unenthusiastic about the transportation and oil plans developed in the summer and autumn of 1944 as the key to speeding up German collapse. 617 Squadron was kept in being for specialist operations, however, and was later used to carry Barnes Wallis's super-heavy bombs which sank the German battleship *Tirpitz* and penetrated the six-metre (20-foot) reinforced concrete roofs of the submarine pens at Brest.

The operational success of the attack on the dams was exploited for propaganda purposes. Guy Gibson, the commander of the operation, was sent on a publicity tour of the United States and the raid attracted a high level of attention in Britain in the summer of 1943. Nevertheless, its strategic worth was limited and the cost in skilled crewmen very great. There was also discussion of its moral implications, which almost certainly made further similar attacks difficult to justify. In postwar international law the deliberate attack of civilian water supplies has been prohibited.

WING COMMANDER GUY GIBSON (1918–44)

The commander of RAF 617 squadron was Wing Commander Guy Gibson. He joined the RAF in 1936 and on the outbreak of war was a pilot in 83rd Squadron, Bomber Command. He survived his first tour of duty and then transferred to Fighter Command where he flew night-fighters. He rejoined Bomber Command in 1942, flying the new Lancaster bombers, and was chosen in early 1943 to command the unit created to attack the German dams. He flew a remarkable 174 operations with Bomber Command, but was killed when his aircraft developed a fuel fault and crashed in the Netherlands on 19 September 1944. He had a reputation for tough professionalism and bravery and took risks other pilots might not have taken. He was awarded the Victoria Cross for his role in the destruction of the dams.

LEFT: Three separate frames show an aircraft of 617 squadron practising dropping the "bouncing bomb" at the Reculver bombing range in Kent, southern England.

ABOVE: Water pours through the broken dam wall of the Möhne Dam after the successful attack. The result was a flood extending some 80 kilometres (50 miles).

9 JULY–1 OCTOBER 1943

THE INVASIONS OF SICILY AND ITALY

It was agreed at the Casablanca Conference that the invasion of Sicily would follow the defeat of the Axis in North Africa.

Planning began in the spring for Operation "Husky", which was assigned to General Alexander's 15th Army Group, made up of Montgomery's 8th Army and Patton's 1st US Armored Corps (renamed 7th US Army for the invasion). The object was to land in force on the southern and southeastern coast and to sweep up the island quickly enough to prevent Axis forces from escaping to the mainland. The date was set for 10 July 1943.

In order to render the ambitious amphibious operation more secure – it was second in size only to the later invasion of France – a risky deception plan was mounted codenamed Operation "Mincemeat" which involved leaving a dead body dressed in the uniform of a Royal Marines major off the Spanish coast with false Allied plans concealed in a briefcase. The body was handed to the British consul, but the briefcase was kept by the Spanish authorities and its contents revealed to the German consul. The fake plan described an Allied operation against Greece with Sicily as a diversion. The ruse worked perfectly and German forces were strengthened in Greece and Sardinia, but not in Sicily.

OPPOSITE: The British 51st Highland Division unloading supplies on a beach in southeast Sicily on 10 July 1943 as part of the invasion force. There was little opposition at first against the British sector.

RIGHT: Badge of the British 6th Airborne Divisions.

Air power was to play an important part in the invasion. In June, an Italian garrison on the island of Pantelleria, lying on the route from North Africa to Sicily, was so pulverized by bombing that the garrison surrendered without an invasion. Aircraft neutralized any threat from Axis air forces during the invasion. On 9 July, the operation began with American and British paratroop landings to secure vital bridges and communications. Strong winds produced a disaster, with 200 British paratroopers drowning in the sea. Out of 2,781 US paratroops, only 200 arrived at the objective near the Sicilian port of Licata. During the night of 9/10 July, a flotilla of 2,590 ships and landing craft approached Sicily, carrying 180,000 men. They were faced by approximately 50,000 German and 270,000 Italian troops, but it was expected that most Italians would have little stomach for the battle.

British forces landed without difficulty on the beaches at Avola and Pachino, and US forces faced serious opposition only at Gela, where the Hermann Göring Division was stationed. Within five days, Allied forces had pushed inland to a line from Agrigento to the Gulf of Catania. Progress proved slow in mountainous terrain which gave every advantage to the defender against an armoured attack. Patton was supposed to protect the flank of the 8th Army as it struck north to Messina and northwest to the central Sicilian city of Enna, but the collapse of Italian resistance against his aggressive armoured drive persuaded him that the whole of the west of the island could fall quickly into Allied hands. This was one of many arguments that continued to sour Anglo-American co-operation. Alexander reluctantly agreed, and Patton's units reached Palermo on 22 July.

Montgomery's progress proved frustratingly slow and Catania was taken only on 5 August. By this time, Alexander had ordered Patton's forces to swing east towards Messina to assist the 1st Canadian Division as it looped west of Mount Etna, on a trajectory initially assigned to the American zone. In the midst of the final push towards Messina, the Italian dictator, Benito Mussolini, was overthrown on 25 July 1943. Hitler, who had insisted on no withdrawal, was compelled to order an evacuation across the Straits of Messina. The Italian army under General Alfredo Guzzoni saw little point in continued resistance. By

OPERATION "HUSKY", 9 JULY–17 AUGUST 1943

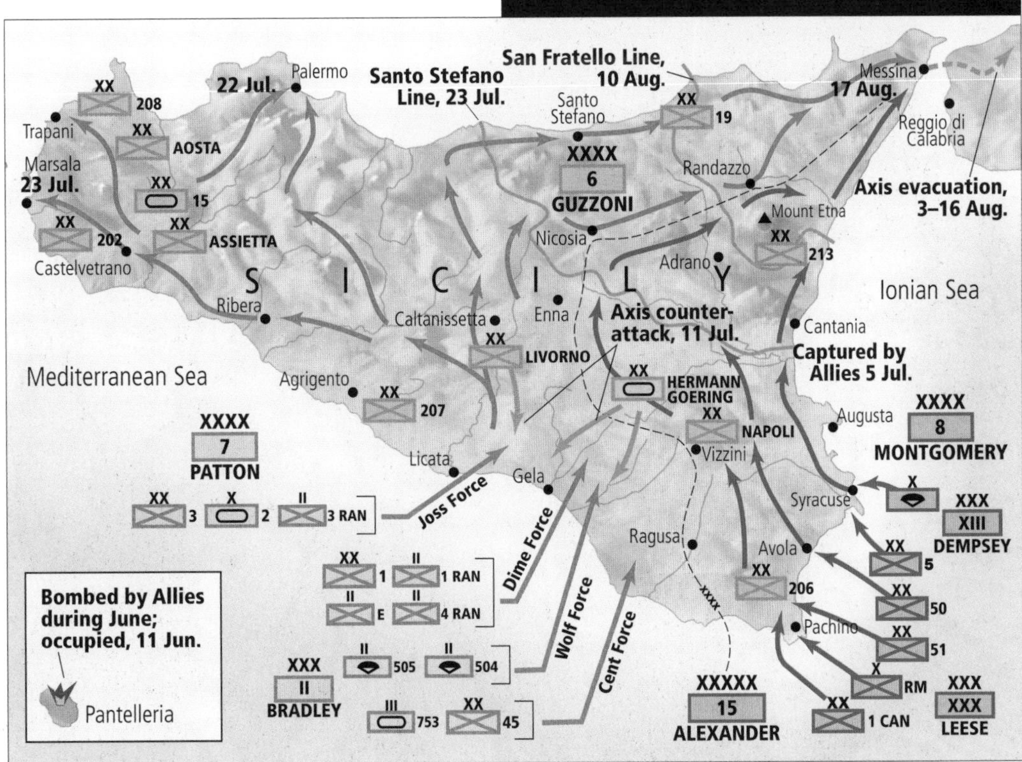

the time Allied forces converged on Messina, over 100,000 Italian and German forces had successfully been removed, without any serious air or naval action by the Allies. Patton arrived in the centre of Messina two hours before the British on 17 August, but the trap had failed to be sprung and one-third of Axis forces escaped. The campaign cost the Allies 38,000 casualties, but approximately 200,000 Italian soldiers surrendered in the course of the campaign, no longer willing to fight for a cause that had collapsed.

The decision to invade Italy after the conquest of Sicily in August 1943 was accelerated by the fall of Mussolini's regime on 25 July. The Allies hoped to be able to capitalize on the change in government to take Italy out of the war before the Germans could reinforce the peninsula adequately. Negotiations with the new regime of Marshal Badoglio were slow to produce a result. On 3 September the Italian armistice was signed at Cassibile, but by that point the Germans had succeeded in strengthening their forces in Italy from six to 18 divisions. It was essential for German strategy that the Allies should be kept as far south as possible, to avoid the establishment of airfields for the bombing of southern Germany and to make it impossible to use Italy as a military roadway into German-occupied Europe.

By the time the armistice was formally announced on 8 September, the Allies had already begun to move onto the Italian mainland. The plan was to land substantial forces in the Gulf of Salerno, south of Naples, and then to move northwards rapidly to take Naples and Rome and south to take over the Italian "heel and toe". Lieutenant

General Mark Clark was put in command of the US 5th Army, consisting of the US 6th Corps and the British 10th Corps, which would land on either side of the River Sele which flowed into the gulf. Before this operation, Montgomery took part of the 8th Army across the Straits of Messina to land unopposed on the morning of 3 September, shortly before the armistice came into effect. The 8th Army then began to push up through Calabria with the eventual aim of meeting up with the forces sent ashore at Salerno.

The situation in Italy was chaotic following the declaration of the armistice; Badoglio, the king and the General Staff fled south to join the Allies, leaving no orders for the large Italian army. German forces immediately disarmed Italian soldiers, but in some cases they resisted, only to be brutally treated and shot out of hand. Some 650,000 Italian soldiers were sent as POWs to Germany, where they became forced labourers. The Italian fleet fled to Malta, but was hit by the German air force with new remote-controlled bombs and the battleship Roma was sunk. The country was divided in two, the far south governed by Badoglio together with the Allies, the north by a new Fascist Italian Social Republic, based in the town of Salò on the shores of Lake Garda, with Mussolini as its nominal leader but the German authorities under Field Marshal Kesselring the real rulers.

On 9 September, Clark's task force sailed for Salerno, already aware that the landing would be strongly resisted by the German occupiers. A fleet of 627 ships arrived off the coast and the naval vessels subjected the coastal area to a fierce bombardment. The British forces under Lieutenant General McCreery landed to the north of the Gulf of Salerno and the Americans under Major General Dawley in the south; although small bridgeheads were secured, shortages of air support and the stiff resistance of the Panzer divisions assigned to the German defence led to a dangerous situation by 12 September, as General von Vietinghoff's growing force began a powerful counter-offensive.

The Allies began to plan for evacuation, but the 82nd US Airborne Division was dropped into the danger zone, while aircraft and extra naval vessels were drafted in to bombard the enemy, and by 16 September German forces began to pull back. By 20 September, the rest of the 8th Army, making its way against much lighter opposition from Taranto and Bari, established firm contact with the Salerno beachhead. The German force pulled back to a prepared line north of Naples, and the port was occupied by Allied forces on 1 October. The scene was now set for a long and bitter campaign through difficult mountain country along the whole length of the Italian peninsula.

OPPOSITE: British troops and vehicles of the 8th Army's 46th Division unload on the beach at Salerno, 9 September 1943. After meeting light resistance at first, the bridgehead came under heavy attack.

ABOVE LEFT: Amphibious DUKWs, known as "ducks", enter the water at Messina in Sicily to cross the narrow straits to mainland Italy on 3 September 1943 during Operation "Baytown".

ABOVE RIGHT: The forward 380-millimetre (15-inch) guns of the British battleship HMS *Warspite* bombarding the Italian coast at Reggio during the early stages of the Allied landings on the mainland of southern Italy. Naval power played an important part in supporting ground operations in the Italian campaign.

24 JULY–2 AUGUST 1943

THE BOMBING OF HAMBURG

In the spring of 1943, RAF Bomber Command chose Hamburg, Germany's second-largest city and a major port and manufacturing centre, for a sustained and destructive attack codenamed Operation "Gomorrah".

The campaign was an opportunity to try out two tactical innovations. The first was a new navigation aid, the H2S radar scanning apparatus that provided an image of the ground, the second a device known as "Window" which would block German radar by distributing thousands of aluminium-coated foil strips to create a mass of confusing data on the radar screen. The orders for "Gomorrah" went out on 27 May and the campaign against Hamburg was scheduled to begin on 24 July.

The attack on Hamburg was planned as a series of operations to maximize destruction and dislocation and to make it difficult for the rescue and fire services to continue to operate effectively. It was a combined operation, the RAF bombing by night and the United States 8th Air Force by day against designated industrial and transport targets. The first attack came on the night of 24/25 July, when 791 bombers set out for the city, the last on the night of 2/3 August when 740 bombers were sent off from British bases. The bomber streams were led by a Pathfinder force which carried H2S equipment and whose task was to pinpoint the main bombing area with flares. During the first operation, around 2,300 tons of bombs were dropped, a mixture of incendiary and high explosive. The following afternoon, 123 American B-17 bombers attacked Hamburg, aiming for the main shipyards. On the night of 25/26 July a handful of British Mosquito bombers flew over Hamburg to create alarm and the following day a further American attack with 121 bombers was made against the port area.

Over the next two days further alarms sounded regularly as the Hamburg population began to leave the city to avoid the continuing threat. On the night of 27/28 July, RAF Bomber Command returned in force with 787 bombers, and it was this raid, which created the first bombing firestorm, that made the operation notorious. The firestorm, in the eastern districts of the city, was the result of the high proportion of incendiary bombs dropped and the difficulty faced by the rescue services, after three days of bombing, in tackling hundreds of fires in areas with blocked roads and disrupted water supplies. The fires gradually merged together and by 1.20 a.m. the storm began to develop, reaching a climax at around 3.00 a.m. with temperatures of 1,800 degrees centigrade and winds of 240 kilometres (150 miles) per hour. Everything in the path of the firestorm was consumed and human bodies incinerated. In the cellars, where many people had fled, the heat literally melted their bodies. The firestorm was the most deadly bombing attack yet experienced and an estimated 40–45,000 people lost their lives in one night, the equivalent of all those killed in nine months of the Blitz against Britain.

Even though Hamburg was now a skeleton city, the RAF returned on the night of 29/30 July, creating a smaller firestorm in the northeast of the city, and once more on the night of 2/3 August, although on this occasion heavy thunderstorms scattered the force and Hamburg suffered much less. On this final raid, the bomber force suffered its

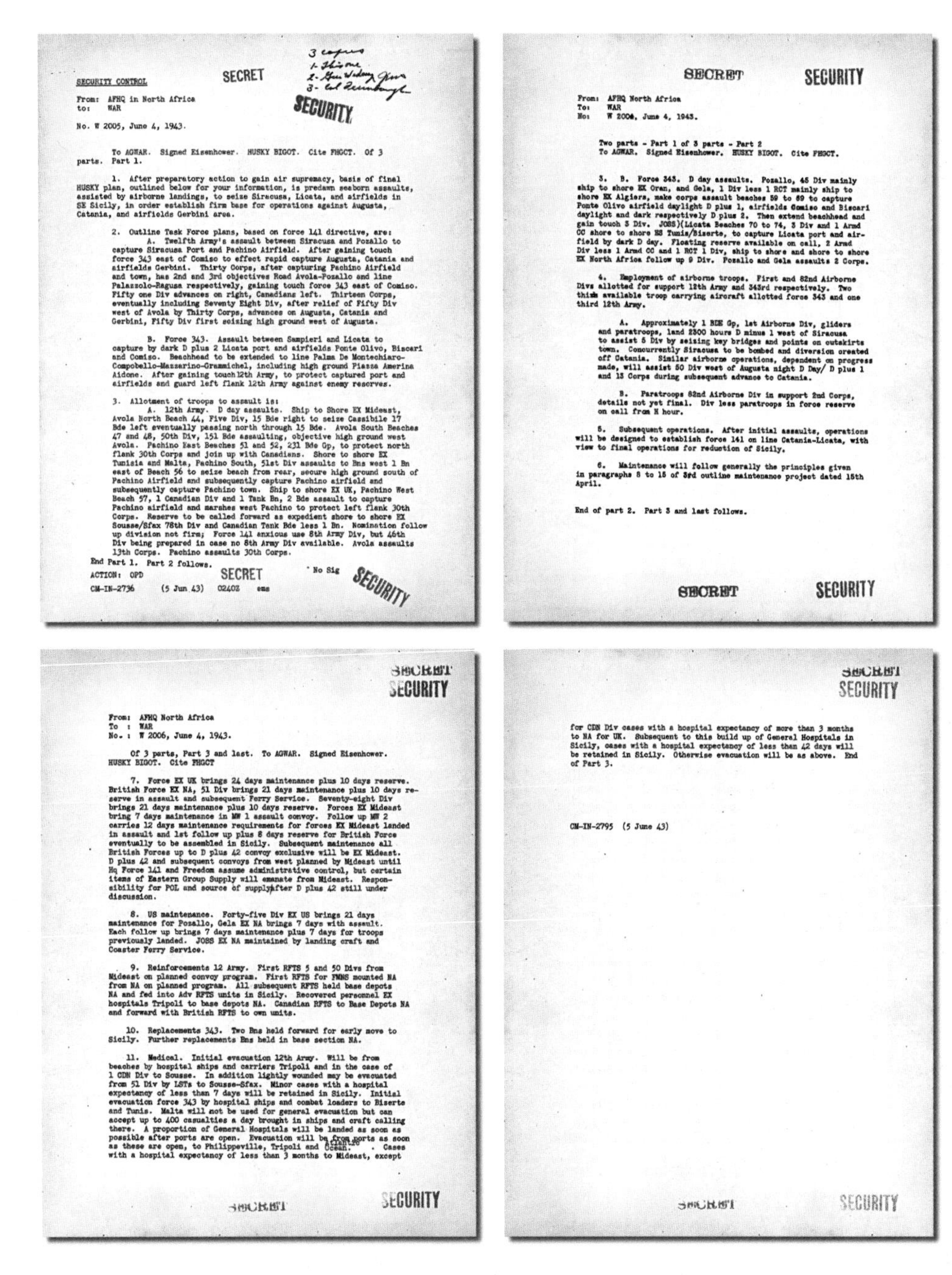

SECURITY CONTROL

SECRET

SECURITY

From: AFHQ in North Africa
to: WAR

No. W 2005, June 4, 1943.

To AGWAR. Signed Eisenhower. HUSKY BIGOT. Cite FHGCT. Of 3 parts. Part 1.

1. After preparatory action to gain air supremacy, basis of final HUSKY plan, outlined below for your information, is predawn seaborn assaults, assisted by airborne landings, to seize Siracusa, Licata, and airfields in SE Sicily, in order establish firm base for operations against Augusta, Catania, and airfields Gerbini area.

2. Outline Task Force plans, based on force 141 directive, are:

A. Twelfth Army's assault between Siracusa and Pozallo to capture Siracusa Port and Pachino Airfield. After gaining touch force 343 east of Comiso to effect rapid capture Augusta, Catania and airfields Gerbini. Thirty Corps, after capturing Pachino Airfield and town, has 2nd and 3rd objectives Road Avola-Pozallo and line Palazzolo-Ragusa respectively, gaining touch force 343 east of Comiso. Fifty one Div advances on right, Canadians left. Thirteen Corps, eventually including Seventy Eight Div, after relief of Fifty Div west of Avola by Thirty Corps, advances on Augusta, Catania and Gerbini, Fifty Div first seizing high ground west of Augusta.

B. Force 343. Assault between Sampieri and Licata to capture by dark D plus 2 Licata port and airfields Ponte Olivo, Biscari and Comiso. Beachhead to be extended to line Palma De Montechiaro-Compobello-Mazzarino-Grammichel, including high ground Piazza Amerina Aidone. After gaining touch 12th Army, to protect captured port and airfields and guard left flank 12th Army against enemy reserves.

3. Allotment of troops to assault is:

A. 12th Army. D day assaults. Ship to Shore EX Mideast, Avola North Beach 44, Five Div, 15 Bde right to seize Cassibile 17 Bde left eventually passing north through 15 Bde. Avola South Beaches 47 and 48, 50th Div, 151 Bde assaulting, objective high ground west Avola. Pachino East Beaches 51 and 52, 231 Bde Gp, to protect north flank 30th Corps and join up with Canadians. Shore to shore EX Tunisia and Malta, Pachino South, 51st Div assaults to Bns west 1 Bn east of Beach 56 to seize beach from rear, secure high ground south of Pachino Airfield and subsequently capture Pachino airfield and subsequently capture Pachino town. Ship to shore EX UK, Pachino West Beach 57, 1 Canadian Div and 1 Tank Bn, 2 Bde assault to capture Pachino airfield and marshes west Pachino to protect left flank 30th Corps. Reserve to be called forward as expedient shore to shore EX Sousse/Sfax 78th Div and Canadian Tank Bde less 1 Bn. Nomination follow up division not firm; Force 141 anxious use 8th Army Div, but 46th Div being prepared in case no 8th Army Div available. Avola assaults 13th Corps. Pachino assaults 30th Corps.

End Part 1. Part 2 follows.

ACTION: OPD SECRET No Sig

CM-IN-2736 (5 Jun 43) 0240Z ems

SECURITY

SECRET SECURITY

From: AFHQ North Africa
To: WAR
No: W 2004, June 4, 1943.

Two parts - Part 1 of 3 parts - Part 2
To AGWAR. Signed Eisenhower. HUSKY BIGOT. Cite FHGCT.

3. B. Force 343. D day assaults. Pozallo, 45 Div mainly ship to shore EX Oran, and Gela, 1 Div less 1 RCT mainly ship to shore EX Algiers, make corps assault beaches 59 to 69 to capture Ponte Olivo airfield daylight D plus 1, airfields Comiso and Biscari daylight and dark respectively D plus 2. Then extend beachhead and gain touch 5 Div. JOSS)(Licata Beaches 70 to 74, 3 Div and 1 Armd CC shore to shore ES Tunis/Bizerte, to capture Licata port and airfield by dark D day. Floating reserve available on call, 2 Armd Div less 1 Armd CC and 1 RCT 1 Div, ship to shore and shore to shore EX North Africa follow up 9 Div. Pozallo and Gela assaults 2 Corps.

4. Employment of airborne troops. First and 82nd Airborne Divs allotted for support 12th Army and 343rd respectively. Two thirds available troop carrying aircraft allotted force 343 and one third 12th Army.

A. Approximately 1 BDE Gp, 1st Airborne Div, gliders and paratroops, land 2300 hours D minus 1 west of Siracusa to assist 5 Div by seizing key bridges and points on outskirts town. Concurrently Siracusa to be bombed and diversion created off Catania. Similar airborne operations, dependent on progress made, will assist 50 Div west of Augusta night D Day/ D plus 1 and 13 Corps during subsequent advance to Catania.

B. Paratroops 82nd Airborne Div in support 2nd Corps, details not yet final. Div less paratroops in force reserve on call from H hour.

5. Subsequent operations. After initial assaults, operations will be designed to establish force 141 on line Catania-Licata, with view to final operations for reduction of Sicily.

6. Maintenance will follow generally the principles given in paragraphs 8 to 15 of 3rd outline maintenance project dated 15th April.

End of part 2. Part 3 and last follows.

SECRET SECURITY

SECRET
SECURITY

From: AFHQ North Africa
To : WAR
No. : W 2006, June 4, 1943.

Of 3 parts, Part 3 and last. To AGWAR. Signed Eisenhower. HUSKY BIGOT. Cite FHGCT

7. Force EX UK brings 24 days maintenance plus 10 days reserve. British Force EX NA, 51 Div brings 21 days maintenance plus 10 days reserve in assault and subsequent Ferry Service. Seventy-eight Div brings 21 days maintenance plus 10 days reserve. Forces EX Mideast bring 7 days maintenance in MW 1 assault convoy. Follow up MW 2 carries 12 days maintenance requirements for forces EX Mideast landed in assault and 1st follow up plus 8 days reserve for British Force eventually to be assembled in Sicily. Subsequent maintenance all British Forces up to D plus 42 convoy exclusive will be EX Mideast. D plus 42 and subsequent convoys from west planned by Mideast until Hq Force 141 and Freedom assume administrative control, but certain items of Eastern Group Supply will emanate from Mideast. Responsibility for POL and source of supply after D plus 42 still under discussion.

8. US maintenance. Forty-five Div EX US brings 21 days maintenance for Pozallo, Gela EX NA brings 7 days with assault. Each follow up brings 7 days maintenance plus 7 days for troops previously landed. JOSS EX NA maintained by landing craft and Coaster Ferry Service.

9. Reinforcements 12 Army. First RFTS 5 and 50 Divs from Mideast on planned convoy program. First RFTS for FMNS mounted NA from NA on planned program. All subsequent RFTS held base depots NA and fed into Adv RFTS units in Sicily. Recovered personnel EX hospitals Tripoli to base depots NA. Canadian RFTS to Base Depots NA and forward with British RFTS to own units.

10. Replacements 343. Two Bns held forward for early move to Sicily. Further replacements Bns held in base section NA.

11. Medical. Initial evacuation 12th Army. Will be from beaches by hospital ships and carriers Tripoli and in the case of 1 CDN Div to Sousse. In addition lightly wounded may be evacuated from 51 Div by LSTs to Sousse-Sfax. Minor cases with a hospital expectancy of less than 7 days will be retained in Sicily. Initial evacuation force 343 by hospital ships and combat loaders to Bizerte and Tunis. Malta will not be used for general evacuation but can accept up to 400 casualties a day brought in ships and craft calling there. A proportion of General Hospitals will be landed as soon as possible after ports are open. Evacuation will be from ports as soon as these are open, to Philippeville, Tripoli and Atlantic Ocean. Cases with a hospital expectancy of less than 3 months to Mideast, except

SECRET SECURITY

SECRET
SECURITY

for CDN Div cases with a hospital expectancy of more than 3 months to NA for UK. Subsequent to this build up of General Hospitals in Sicily, cases with a hospital expectancy of less than 42 days will be retained in Sicily. Otherwise evacuation will be as above. End of Part 3.

CM-IN-2795 (5 June 43)

SECRET SECURITY

OPPOSITE: American Boeing B-17 "Flying Fortress" bombers in formation on a mission over Germany. The heavily armed bomber formed the mainstay of the US 8th Air Force bomber squadrons stationed in England and was used in the raids on Hamburg on 25 and 26 July 1943.

RIGHT: The final plan for Operation "Husky", drawn up on 4-5 June 1943 following the defeat of Axis forces in Tunisia in May. Eisenhower remained the overall commander-in-chief while the British general Harold Alexander took command of forces in the field.

highest losses, 30 aircraft in total. Over the whole campaign the RAF dropped approximately 7,800 tons of bombs on Hamburg for the loss of 87 bombers, while the two 8th Air Force raids cost 17 bombers. The damage to the city was extensive: 25 square kilometres (10 square miles) of the city were obliterated, leaving over one million people homeless. Half the city's 81,000 commercial and industrial buildings were destroyed and over 40,000 residential buildings. Losses also included 58 churches, 277 schools and 24 hospitals. Besides the 45,000 dead were 37,439 with serious injuries.

The economic impact on Hamburg was, however, much less than Harris and Bomber Command had hoped. By the end of 1943, Hamburg's industrial production had reached 82 per cent of the pre-raid level. Much of the damage had been to residential areas, but local war industries, while temporarily disrupted by the exodus of workers from the city, were quickly restored or dispersed to safer sites. Albert Speer, the German armaments minister, thought that six similar attacks would knock Germany out of the war, but Bomber Command proved unable to replicate "Gomorrah".

26 DECEMBER 1943

BATTLE OF THE NORTH CAPE

The Battle of the North Cape, fought on Boxing Day (26 December) 1943, was the last engagement fought by the Royal Navy against a major battleship.

The battle had its origins in the decision by the British government in November 1943 to recommence the Arctic aid convoys to the Soviet Union, which had been suspended in March 1943 because of the threat posed by German air and sea power and shortages of naval shipping. The two large German ships in Norwegian waters, the battleship *Tirpitz* and the fast battlecruiser *Scharnhorst*, had in fact done very little for most of the war and Hitler had decided that they should be scrapped. The resumption of northern convoys encouraged the German navy commander-in-chief Admiral Dönitz to order an attack so that Hitler could be shown that the large ships were not simply a waste of resources.

On 20 December, a large convoy, JW55B, left Loch Ewe in Scotland bound for the Soviet Arctic ports. An empty convoy, RA55A, was returning the other way. The two convoys would cross in the strait between Bear Island and the North Cape in northern Norway. The commander of

OPPOSITE: The snow-covered forward gun turrets of the British cruiser HMS *Belfast* during a patrol in Arctic waters. The Belfast was on patrol near North Cape when the *Scharnhorst* left Norway to intercept two British convoys.

RIGHT: Blindfolded survivors of the sinking of the *Scharnhorst* are led ashore at the British naval base of Scapa Flow. Out of a crew of 2,000, only 36 survived.

BELOW: The German battleship *Tirpitz* at her berth on the Norwegian coast under air attack on 3 April 1943. Despite regular attacks from bombers the battleship remained resistant to all attempts to sink her until November 1944, though the bombing severely disabled the ship and prevented the remains of the German battle fleet fighting together.

the British Home Fleet, Admiral Fraser, suspected from intelligence evidence that the German navy would attempt to intercept the convoys, and on 23 December he took his flagship, the battleship *Duke of York*, with 360-millimetre (14-inch) guns, out to sea with a strong escort of one cruiser and four destroyers. To the east was a cruiser group under Vice Admiral Robert Burnett of *Belfast*, *Norfolk* and *Sheffield* which could also be used to defend the convoy and engage any German units.

The German commander of the *Scharnhorst*, Vice Admiral Bey, was a temporary appointment whose previous experience had been confined to destroyers. Encouraged by Dönitz to take action, the German headquarters at Kiel ordered Bey to take out his ships on Christmas Day 1943 and intercept a convoy, whose whereabouts were not known precisely, nor the position or strength of any Royal Navy force that might be protecting it. The weather was atrocious, with heavy squally snow showers and high seas, but Bey left the safety of his fjord together with four destroyers. By the morning of 26 December, Bey had lost contact with his covering force and never regained it. Instead, the battlecruiser sailed on towards the convoy on its own, and into the path of the waiting British cruiser squadron. The *Scharnhorst* was detected by radar and then visibly and at 9.30 a.m. *Norfolk* began to engage, knocking out Bey's forward radar. The German ship made off to the north, towards the convoy.

The attack was a complete surprise for the German ship, but Bey relied on superior speed to reach the convoy ahead of the cruisers. Burnett took a shorter route and just after midday contact was restored and the attack began again. This time the cruisers were damaged by the heavier shells of the battlecruiser, but Bey decided that the risk of attacking the convoy was now too great and turned for base, straight into the path of Fraser's force which was placed between the German ship and the Norwegian coast. Poor intelligence and reconnaissance left Bey in ignorance of the trap until, at 4.48 p.m., a salvo from the *Duke of York* straddled the *Scharnhorst*. The British battleship fired 52 salvos and damaged the German ship's boiler room, slowing it down to 8–10 knots. The other British ships closed in for the kill, but it took 11 torpedoes before the German ship sank at 7.45 p.m. with the loss of all but 36 of the 2,000-man crew.

The battleship *Tirpitz* stayed in Norwegian waters and, following 22 attacks by aircraft, was finally sunk on 12 November 1944 by two "Tallboy" heavy bombs with the loss of 1,204 men. Hitler's lack of confidence in battleships proved to have some foundation.

22 JANUARY–25 MAY 1944

THE BATTLES FOR ANZIO AND MONTE CASSINO

Following the landings at Salerno, the Allies decided on a second coastal landing a little south of Rome around the port of Anzio as a way of turning the German Gustav Line, which by late December 1943 ran from Formia on the west coast to Ortona in the east, a mainly mountainous terrain with narrow river valleys, ideal for defensive purposes.

The Anzio landings, strongly supported by Churchill and organized by General Mark Clark, were designed to trap the German 10th Army, which was resisting the advance of the British 8th Army and the US-led 5th Army towards the mountain stronghold around the ancient monastery of Monte Cassino. It was also hoped that the landings would open the way for an advance to Rome.

The operation, codenamed "Shingle", carried a considerable risk because the forces involved were modest. The 6th US Army Corps under Major General John Lucas comprised the British 1st Infantry Division and the US 3rd Infantry Division, supported by commandos and rangers, and a powerful element of air support. On 22 January 1944, over 370 ships arrived off the Italian coast to be met by no initial resistance. The Allied force landed and established a narrow beachhead, but Lucas, whose immediate objectives had not been made entirely clear in the planning, dug his forces in rather than exploiting the advantage of tactical surprise. Though often criticized for the decision, it almost certainly saved the operation from disaster, for within four days Field Marshal Kesselring succeeded in improvising a six-division 14th Army under General von Mackensen, which on 1 February began a sustained assault on the perimeter of the Anzio area after a number of smaller forays.

Although Lucas was soon reinforced, and was strongly supported by air and sea bombardment, the German forces

LEFT: A Sherman tank and armoured personnel carriers on the beach at Anzio on 22 January 1944. The initial landings met almost no resistance, unlike the landings at Salerno, but German forces soon regrouped and counter-attacked.

LEFT: Allied shipping unloading supplies in Anzio harbour in mid-February 1944. The bridgehead was held thanks to a regular flow of materiel and reinforcements, which could be brought in by sea with a small level of risk.

ABOVE: Badge of the 56th London Infantry Division.

BELOW: British soldiers shelter in a trench from German shelling on 22 May 1944, shortly before the breakout from the Anzio bridgehead, which opened the road to Rome.

succeeded in containing the bridgehead in five months of bitter fighting. By mid-February, the German counter-offensive threatened to drive a salient into the Allied line, dividing the British to the north of Anzio from the Americans to the south. Probing attacks by German armoured forces pushed back British and American troops, who had begun a cautious move out from their initial defensive line. A salient formed by the British 1st Division was attacked and on 9 February the 3rd Panzer Grenadier Division recaptured Aprilia and two days later the Scots Guards were expelled from the town of Carroceto, captured on 25 January. Von Mackensen was instructed by Kesselring to concentrate his forces for a major offensive, codenamed "Fischfang" (Fish-catch) to divide the bridgehead and then expel it.

The Allies were pre-warned by ULTRA intelligence and a heavy air bombardment was directed at the German concentrations, but on 16 February von Mackensen launched a strong attack at the weak line between the British and American sectors which was only halted by a further ferocious barrage of fire from sea, air and artillery. The Germans established a salient eight kilometres (five miles) wide and three kilometres (two miles) deep but could progress no further. Six days later, Lucas was redeployed and his deputy, Major General Lucian Truscott, placed in effective command. His first action was to tour the battlefield, visiting every one of the Allied units in an effort to boost sagging morale. A second major German attack on 29 February was also repulsed. What followed was a war of attrition between the two sides: the German ring of armoured divisions was never quite powerful enough to push the bridgehead back into the sea, but the 6th Corps, despite continuous reinforcement, was too weak to break the cordon.

The trench stalemate was broken only by renewed pressure on the Gustav Line from Allied forces around Cassino. It became clear to Kesselring that the line would not hold, and German forces prepared to withdraw to defensive lines prepared further up the Italian peninsula. As the German grip weakened, Truscott prepared a fresh offensive and on 23 May Allied forces broke out of the Anzio

RIGHT: A photograph of the Benedictine monastery of Monte Cassino taken c.1927. The site had been a monastery since the 6th century AD and was a building of exceptional architectural and religious significance. German forces promised not to occupy the building and did not do so until it had been destroyed by Allied bombing.

OPPOSITE ABOVE: Troops of the Polish 2nd Corps climbing the slopes of the monastery hill in May 1944. The Polish units took terrible casualties in the assault but fought with exceptional courage.

OPPOSITE BELOW: Polish and British flags fly side by side above the monastery of Monte Cassino on 18 May 1944 after the German withdrawal. The capture of Monte Cassino paved the way for a rapid advance past Rome to Florence.

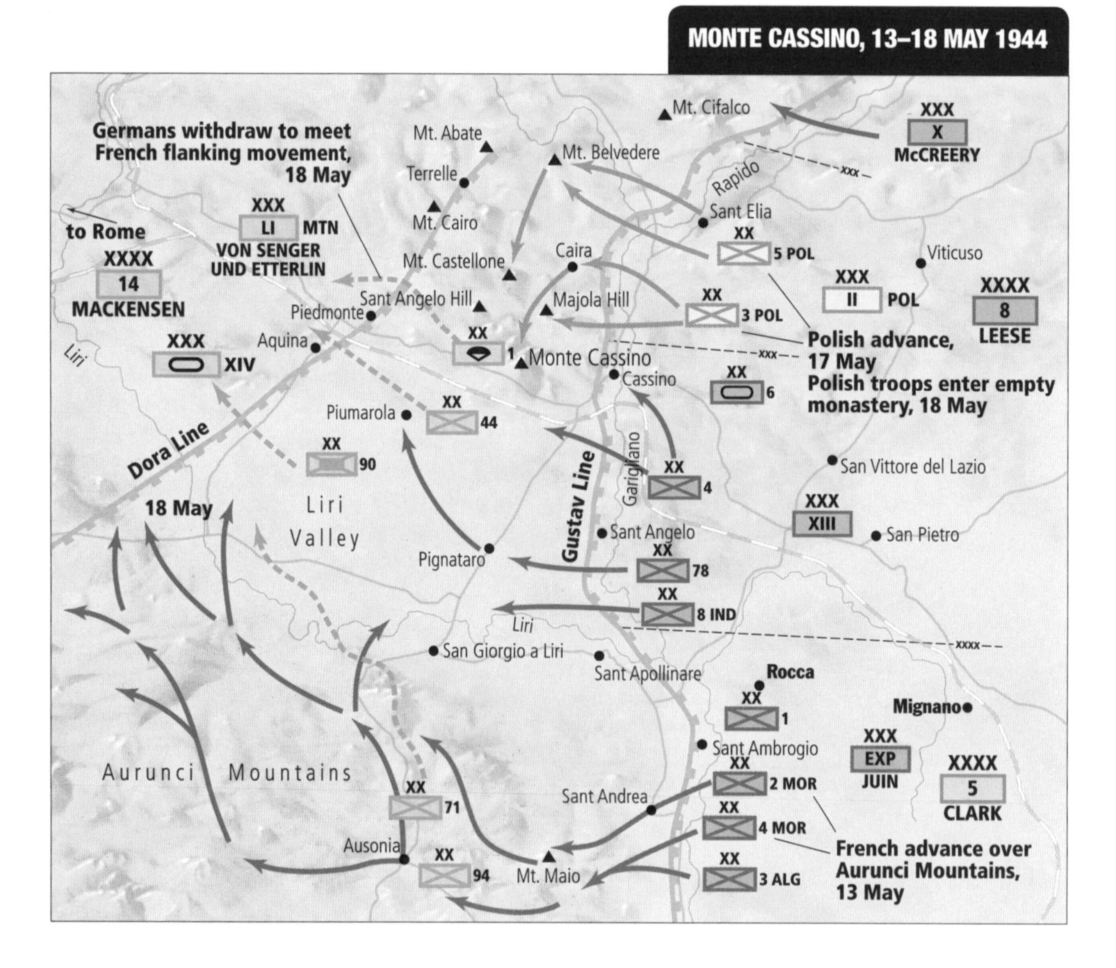

bridgehead and drove east, intending to encircle the retreating Germans. Instead General Clark ordered a drive northwards, and Rome fell on 4 June to American forces. The costs of the Anzio campaign were high, 43,000 for the Allies, including 7,000 dead, and an estimated 40,000 for the Germans, with 5,000 killed.

The key to breaking the German grip on south central Italy was the heavily defended area around Cassino and the valleys of the Liri and Rapido rivers.

This was the setting for one of the most bitterly contested struggles of the war in the west which led to the complete destruction of the ancient Benedictine monastery of Monte Cassino, set high on an outcrop of mountainside above the town of Cassino.

The battle for Cassino lasted five months and involved four major operations. The German 14th Panzer Corps, under General von Senger und Etterlin, bore the brunt of the defence, dug in to the rugged landscape and valley sides that made up this part of the Gustav Line. The Allied plan, set out in a directive from Alexander's headquarters on 8 November 1943, was to destroy German forces in the Liri valley and to approach Rome from the south, in conjunction with a landing at Anzio designed to roll up the German front. Early attacks in December on the German defences showed how difficult the assault would be with Allied forces that were battle-worn after the hard drive up from Sicily.

The opening battle began on 17 January 1944 when British forces tried to cross the River Garigliano and the Americans the River Rapido three days later. Small bridgeheads were secured against fierce resistance and the US 5th Army began a slow ascent towards the monastery before heavy losses forced a halt on mountains to the northeast while the French Expeditionary Corps made progress to the north. But on 11 February the first attack was called off, with total Allied casualties of 14,000, sustained in weeks of harsh weather and fierce fighting. A second assault was planned a week later using General Freyberg's New Zealand Corps, but Freyberg, anxious that German troops would use the monastery as a fortress, requested a preliminary bombing attack. Clark was unwilling, but he was overruled by Alexander, the Allied commander in Italy. On 15 February, 229 bombers pulverized the monastery into ruins.

It was only then that the German forces moved into the rubble, which provided good defensive positions. The only inhabitants of the monastery had been Italian civilians and a number of monks sheltering from the conflict, and between 300 and 400 were killed. On 15 February, the New Zealanders attacked the Cassino railway station while the 4th Indian Division attacked the monastery hill. After three days the offensive was called off after achieving almost nothing. Alexander then planned to wait until the spring to launch a more carefully prepared assault, but under pressure from London and Washington to give relief to the threatened Anzio beachhead, a third assault on Cassino was tried. After a massive air bombardment which turned Cassino into a ruin, the New Zealand Corps again tried to storm the town between 15 and 23 March, but after taking 4,000 casualties and battered by appalling weather, the attack was called off.

The final assault was postponed until May. Alexander prepared a major operation, codenamed "Diadem", designed finally to unhinge the German line. The French forces in the south pushed across the Garigliano River and the Aurunci Mountains, threatening the whole south of the German line. The British 8th Army assaulted and finally captured Cassino, while on 17 May the Polish 2nd Corps under General Anders assaulted the monastery and after heavy hand-to-hand fighting, and losses of 3,500 men, occupied it on 18 May as German forces withdrew. The fourth Cassino battle persuaded Kesselring that his position was untenable and he began moving his forces back to the Gothic Line, north of Florence. Clark's 5th Army met up with Truscott's Anzio forces on 25 May. In the end, victory at Cassino was needed to rescue the Anzio operation, the opposite of what had been intended when the operations to break the Gustav Line were first launched late in 1943.

1939–1945

THE SECRET WAR: SPIES, CODES AND DECEPTION

The secret war of spying, deception code-making and code-breaking played an important part in the conduct of the Second World War for all the combatant powers.

There were two main purposes behind the secret war: to shield from the enemy any knowledge of strategic and operational plans and force strengths, and to find out the plans and force strengths of the enemy. But there was also the possibility, exploited at times with remarkable success, of deceiving the enemy about operational intentions in order to maximize the chances of success and to get the enemy to dispose their forces at a disadvantage.

The most glamorous, but in many ways least successful, aspect of the secret war was spying. Most spies were caught

if they operated in enemy country, and in many cases turned into double agents. In Britain a special double-cross organization, the XX-Committee, was set up under J C Masterman in September 1940 which succeeded in "'turning" a number of German spies and sending back misleading information to the German counter-intelligence organization, the Abwehr. Almost all German spies were caught, but so too were British agents in occupied Europe. The most successful spies were Soviet, but they spied on their allies as well as their enemies. The Communist Red Orchestra spy ring was based in Göring's Air Ministry in Berlin until it was broken in 1942, but Soviet spies in Britain and the United States went undetected for years. The "Cambridge Five" worked at the heart of the British intelligence effort in MI6 and MI5, from where they fed a regular diet of information to their Soviet NKVD controller in London. In the Pacific War, the Allies made little use of spying, but Japanese spy networks in Hawaii and the United States supplied useful information before Pearl Harbor, though little thereafter.

Spying was a risky and unreliable source of information. During the war much more was expected from breaking enemy codes and ciphers. This was done routinely in most theatres, but the important point was to try to conceal from the enemy the fact that the codes had been broken. The Allies had a remarkable success in breaking German and Japanese codes and then preventing that knowledge from filtering back to the German and Japanese armed forces. The German Enigma coding machine, which was thought to be unbreakable, was first read in 1940, though very incompletely, but by the end of the war ULTRA traffic, as the British called it, could be read routinely and quickly. The effort to avoid giving any clue that the Allies could read their secret traffic was a major intelligence operation in its own right, but the Germans assumed that Enigma was unbreakable and that the Allies got their information from other sources. The same was true in the Pacific where Japanese diplomatic traffic (PURPLE or MAGIC) and military traffic (ULTRA) was read by the Americans and the British, giving invaluable advance warning of Japanese moves after the disastrous failure at Pearl Harbor.

The third element of the secret war, deception, was perhaps the most important, because it could affect an entire campaign. The Allies had notable successes. The Soviet deception before the "Uranus" operation in November 1942 or Operation "Bagration" in summer 1944 was complete, and rapid victory in both cases owed a lot to the unpreparedness of Axis forces. The most famous was the "Fortitude" deception before D-Day, when an entirely fictitious army group (FUSAG) was set up in southeast England, with dummy tanks and bogus camps, to persuade Hitler that the assault would come across the narrowest part of the English Channel. A fake order-of-battle was also fed into German intelligence by double agents in Britain and the United States. So realistic was the deception that Hitler ordered large forces to remain in the Pas-de-Calais when they were desperately needed to repel the Normandy landings. British deception plans were carried out with particular skill and success, but this relied on the gullibility of the enemy. The German armed forces were less interested in playing deception games and so were an easy target for British ingenuity. The Allies in general made much greater use of intelligence as an arm of battle than did the Axis.

OPPOSITE: The world's first computer was set up at the British code and cipher school at Bletchley Park to speed up the decrypting of the Enigma messages. Colossus II was in operation from June 1944.

ABOVE: General Heinz Guderian in his command vehicle watches soldiers sending messages using the Enigma machine. Some of the Enigma codes were regularly read by Allied intelligence from the early stages of the war.

7 MARCH—18 JULY 1944

BATTLE FOR INDIA: IMPHAL AND KOHIMA

The Japanese in Burma intended to hold the country defensively to prevent the Allies opening a supply route from India to the Chinese forces fighting in southern China.

But the incursion of Chindit units in spring 1943 persuaded the Japanese commanders that Burma might be made more secure by seizing a frontier zone around Imphal and Kohima in Indian Assam. Lieutenant General Renya Mutaguchi, appointed to command the Japanese 15th Army in Burma in March 1943, used his friendship with the Burma commander-in-chief, General Kawabe, to persuade the Tokyo government to endorse an attack on India, despite strong criticism of an operation in which supply would prove a permanent obstacle.

The Japanese plan for what they called Operation "U-Go" was to seize the main supply depot at Imphal, cut the road from the north at Kohima and then to dig in on the new frontier while monsoon rains prevented

an Allied counter-offensive. As the operation was being prepared, British and Indian forces attacked Arakan in southern Burma and routed a Japanese force there, while in northern Burma General Stilwell, using Chinese forces assisted by the British Chindits and the American "Merrill's Marauders", launched a protracted campaign to try to seize the northern town of Myitkyina. Both operations effectively weakened the Japanese forces prepared for the Imphal-Kohima offensive, but it was possible to organize a total force of between 80,000 and 100,000 men for an operation which opened on 7 March with an attack by the Japanese 33rd Division from the south towards Imphal.

Despite intelligence warnings, the opening of a southern offensive surprised General Slim's 14th Army which made a rapid retreat towards Imphal, leaving the Indian 20th Division stranded and surrounded around Shenam, where it held out against Japanese attacks. Slim airlifted two divisions from Arakan to reinforce the Imphal area and by the time Mutaguchi released the 15th Division towards the town, Slim had been able to organize the first stages of an effective defence. The Japanese force succeeded in cutting the roads to Imphal and there followed a four-month siege during which Slim was supplied by the RAF Third Tactical Air Force, bringing reinforcements, oil, food and military equipment.

Further to the north, Mutaguchi sent the 31st Division under Lieutenant General Kotoku Sato to seize Kohima and open up the possibility of capturing the more distant British supply depot at Dimapur. Struggling through mountainous jungle territory, Sato succeeded in bringing his whole division to Kohima, surrounding the town on 5 April and fighting street by street to capture it. By 18 April, the defenders were confined to one small hill but a relief force sent down the road from Dimapur broke the siege and Sato found his forces pushed slowly back until, on 31 May, he ordered a general withdrawal of his exhausted and poorly supplied troops. The battle was hard fought, bringing 6,000 Japanese casualties but 4,000 British and Indian losses.

Mutaguchi's plan had been for Sato to seize Kohima and then send help south to reinforce the siege of Imphal. The failure further

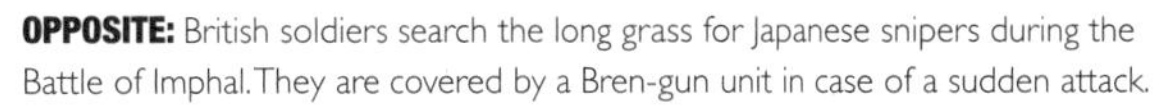
OPPOSITE: British soldiers search the long grass for Japanese snipers during the Battle of Imphal. They are covered by a Bren-gun unit in case of a sudden attack.

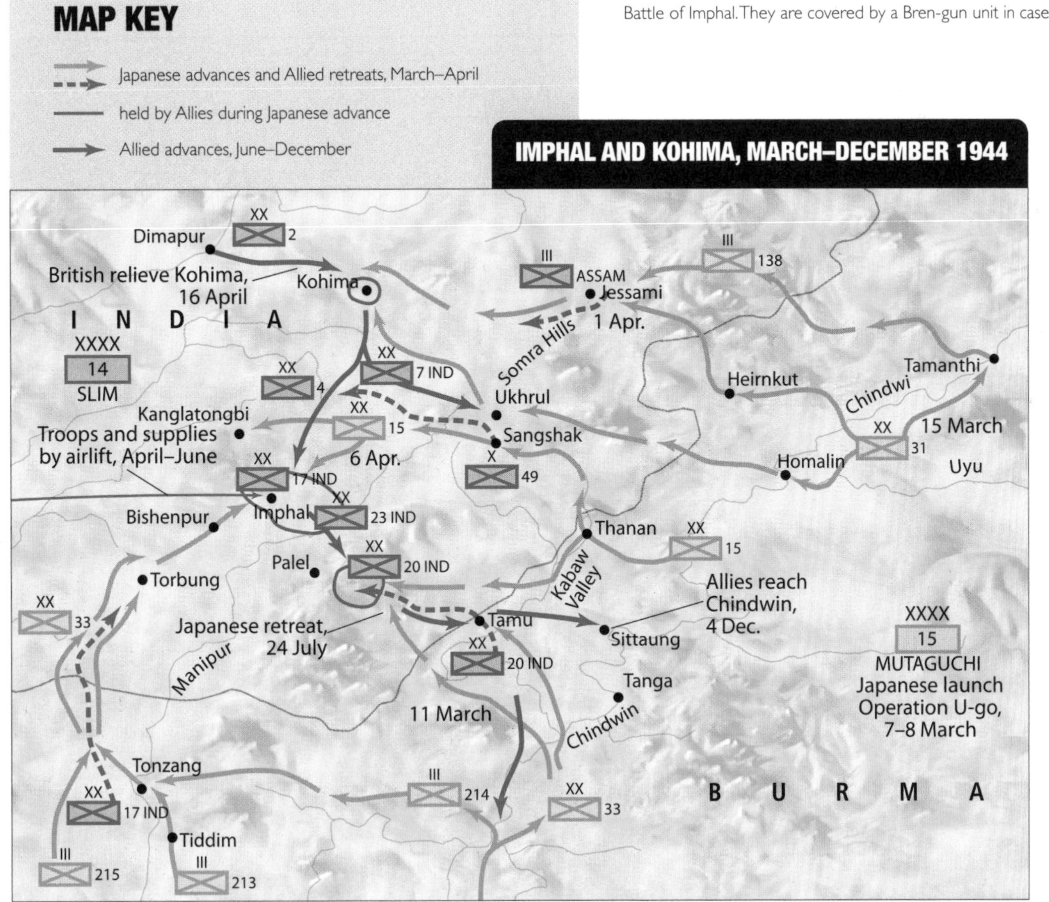

north left the Japanese facing a growing battle of attrition against a surrounded force too heavily armed to be decisively defeated. Slim's forces reopened the road from Imphal to Kohima on 22 June, breaking the siege, while the Japanese, short of food, ammunition and heavy equipment, and wracked with disease, fought an increasingly suicidal campaign. On 18 July, Kawabe and Mutaguchi agreed to terminate the operation and began a withdrawal that turned into a disastrous retreat as Slim's strengthened army pursued them across the Chindwin River. Japanese losses were 53,000, including at least 30,000 killed. The campaign broke the back of Japanese military strength in Burma and paved the way for the reconquest of the country in 1945.

RIGHT: Japanese soldiers in the ruins of a building during Operation "U-Go" against Kohima and Imphal. The Japanese forces were poorly supplied and took heavy losses during the campaign.

BELOW: Men of the West Yorkshire Regiment clear a Japanese roadblock on the road between Imphal and Kohima during the Japanese offensive in 1944.

ABOVE: Badge of the British 14th Army formed in November 1943 to defend India and Burma.

BELOW: A Japanese position under fire on the Tamu Road. British Empire forces had a considerable advantage in tanks and aircraft over the Japanese attackers.

GENERAL MASAKAZU KAWABE (1886–1965)

In March 1943, General Kawabe was made commander-in-chief of the Burma Area Army. A graduate of the army college in 1907, Kawabe was an infantry commander and in 1929–32 military attaché in Berlin. He was involved in the Marco Polo Bridge incident that sparked the Sino-Japanese war in July 1937, and became chief-of-staff of the Central China Expeditionary Army in 1938–39 and again in 1942–43. In Burma in 1944, he approved plans to invade India despite opposition from other senior commanders, but following their failure he was replaced and sent back to Japan in August that year. He joined the Supreme War Council, was promoted to full general andz commanded first the Central Army District then the Air General Army (made up from all remaining aircraft in Japan) for the defence of the home islands. After helping to demobilize the army after surrender, he retired at the end of 1945.

6 JUNE 1944
D-DAY

The invasion of Normandy on 6 June 1944 was the culmination of years of strategic argument and operational preparation by the two Western Allies, Britain and the United States.

In 1942, the US Army chief, General Marshall, wanted commitment to a cross-Channel Operation "Roundup" in the spring of 1943 following the build-up of American forces in Britain. British leaders were never enthusiastic about this plan and the decision to invade first North Africa (November 1942) and then Sicily (July 1943) made any major operation in northern Europe impossible. In the spring of 1943, a planning staff was finally established under the British Lieutenant General Frederick Morgan to prepare for a possible invasion in May 1944. Over the course of 1943 this option hardened into a definite plan to invade on a narrow front in Normandy, but only at the Quebec Conference in August 1943 was the decision to launch what was called Operation "Overlord" finally confirmed. Over the winter of 1943–44 British leaders still harboured doubts and preferred a more peripheral strategy in the Mediterranean to a head-on collision with German forces in France.

The planning and preparation speeded up after Quebec. General Eisenhower was appointed the supreme commander for "Overlord" and General Bernard Montgomery was chosen as the army commander-in-chief in the field. Both men realized that the original plan to attack on a narrow front with a handful of divisions would not work. The eventual plan foresaw an attack on a broader front with five divisions on five separate beaches, to be followed up with a force of 37 divisions which would break out and defeat the German armies in France. On 1 February, the staff planners agreed on the basis of the tides that 31 May would be D-Day, with an option for 5, 6 or 7 June if the weather proved difficult in May. The problem of supplying the beachhead was solved by the development of artificial harbours or "mulberries" that were to be towed in parts across the Channel and assembled close to the front line. The supply and transportation for D-Day was organized under the naval Operation "Neptune" commanded by the Royal Navy's Admiral Ramsay, who led 7,000 warships, transports and small boats towards the coast of France on the eventual day of the invasion.

To oppose the Allied invasion the German army had constructed a complex web of defences across northern France known as the Atlantic Wall. Command of the

OPPOSITE: British Commandos of 1st Special Service Brigade landing from an LCI(S) (Landing Craft Infantry Small) on "Queen Red" Beach, "Sword" area, at La Brèche, at approximately 8.40 am, 6 June. The brigade commander, Brigadier the Lord Lovat DSO MC, can be seen striding through the water to the right of the column of men. The figure nearest the camera on the right is the brigade's bagpiper, Piper Bill Millin.

RIGHT: Infantry of the British 2nd Army waiting to move off "Queen White" beach, "Sword" area, while under enemy fire on the morning of 6 June. By nightfall the British had 28,850 men ashore and the Orne bridge had been seized.

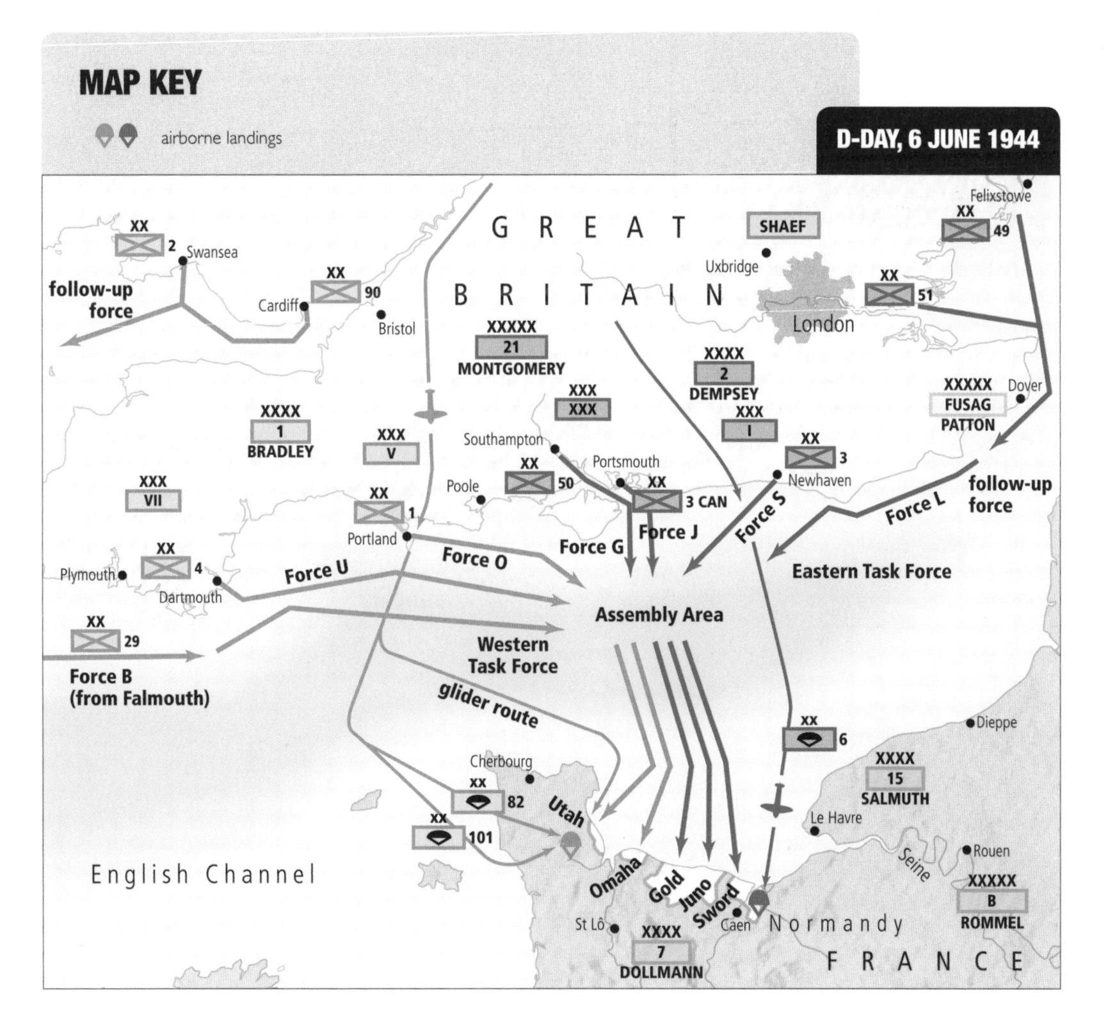

German armies in the field was given to Field Marshal Rommel but his view that the best way to repel invasion was on the beaches clashed with his immediate superior, Field Marshal von Rundstedt, who wanted the mobile forces instead held back from the coast to avoid Allied air and naval power but ready to launch an annihilating counter-offensive. Hitler intervened and divided the mobile forces so that neither strategy could work well, with too few mobile divisions on the coast yet too few in reserve. By June 1944, there were 58 divisions spread out over the whole of France. Rommel expected invasion in the Pas-de-Calais in northeastern France and a diversionary attack in Normandy. Hence, by June 1944 there were 14 divisions in General Dollmann's 7th Army in Normandy, but 20 divisions along the coast around Calais. Thanks to a successful deception plan, planted in German minds by double-agents working in Britain, most German military planners, and Hitler too, expected the main weight of attack across the shortest stretch of Channel towards Calais. When Allied forces finally sailed for Normandy, the German defence was caught almost entirely by surprise.

After months of preparation the date for invasion was fixed in mid-May for 5 June. The United States First Army under Lieutenant General Omar Bradley was to attack two beaches codenamed "Omaha" and "Utah", while the British 2nd Army under Lieutenant General Miles Dempsey attacked "Juno", "Gold" and "Sword" beaches. Poor weather forced postponement until 6 June, but early that morning the huge armada of warships and smaller craft approached the French coast; there then began a ferocious bombardment, first with 2,856 heavy bombers, then with naval gunfire and finally with waves of fighter-bombers. So heavy was the bombardment that in the British sector the fight for the beaches was easily won and by the end of the day a bridgehead several kilometres deep had been

Fernschreibstelle

Geheim

--- S S D -- HZPH 09571 9/6 1850=
AN WEST ROEM 1 C =
GLTD: LEITSTELLE ROEM 1 WEST / PARIS= WEST ROEM 1 C ..-
OB WEST ROEM 1 C= -- G E H E I M --

V- ALARIC-UNTERNEHMEN ARABAL MELDET 9. JUNI AUS ENGLAND:..
NACH PERSOENLICHER RUECKSPRACHE AM 8. JUNI IN LONDON MIT
MEINEN AGENTEN JONNY, DICK UND DORICK , DEREN MELDUNGEN
HEUTE UEBERMITTELT, BIN ICH AUF GRUND DER STARKEN
TRUPPENBEREITSTELLUNGEN IN SUEDOST UND OSTENGLAND, DIE AN
AUGENBLICKLICHEN OPERATIONEN NICHT BETEILIGT SIND, DER
ANSICHT, DASS DIE OPERATIONEN ABLENKUNGSMANOEVER SIND MIT
ZWECK FEINDLICHE RESERVEN AUF SICH ZU ZIEHEN, UM DANN
ENTSCHEIDENDEN STOSS AN ANDERER STELLE ZU FUEHREN.
DIESES KOENNTE UNTER BERUECKSICHTIGUNG DER FORTGESETZTEN
LUFTANGRIFFE AN DER HIER FUER STRATEGISCH GUENSTIGEN LAGE
DES ERWAEHNTEN BEREITSTELLUNGSRAUMES SEHR WOHL IN DER

GEGEND PAS DE CALAIS ERFOLGEN, INSBESONDERE DA BEI EIN
SOLCHEN ANGRIFF DIE NAEHER GELEGENEN LUFTSTUETZPUNKTE
FORTGESETZT STAERKSTE UNTERSTUETZUNG DURCH
LUFTSTREITKRAEFTE EINES SOLCHEN UNTERNEHMENS ERLEICHT
WERDEN.=

RSHA, MIL. AMT, BR B NR 3435/44 G ROEM 1 H WEST / ...

ADMIRAL BERTRAM RAMSAY (1883–1945)

Admiral Ramsay was the naval mastermind behind first the Dunkirk evacuations and then the naval component of the D-Day operations. He joined the Royal Navy in 1898 and served as a lieutenant commander in the Dover Patrol between 1915 and 1918. He retired as a rear admiral in 1938 after disagreements with his immediate superior but was recalled to active duty as flag officer, Dover between August 1939 and 1942. He was deputy naval commander for the "Torch" landings in November 1942, and commander of the Eastern Task Force for the invasion of Sicily before his appointment as Allied naval commander-in-chief for the invasion of France. He was a popular, efficient and tough-minded commander, who achieved remarkable success in organizing the naval back-up for the invasion. He died in an air crash on 2 January 1945.

captured and defended against limited German counter-attacks. American forces had the same success at "Utah", landing against only light fire and carving out a 10-kilometre (six-mile) bridgehead by the end of the day with only 197 casualties. On "Omaha" beach there was a harder battle, since the initial bombardment had failed to hit the defences effectively and high cliffs made rapid movement difficult. By the end of the day the beach was held, but little more; and with around 2,000 casualties. During the day a total of 132,000 men were landed successfully in Normandy for the overall price of around 10,300 casualties from all causes.

ABOVE LEFT: Royal Marine Commandos attached to 3rd Division for the assault on Sword Beach move inland, 6 June 1944. A Churchill bridgelayer can be seen in the background.

ABOVE RIGHT: "Sword" Beach on the morning of 6 June 1944. Support troops of the 3rd British Infantry Division gather near La Brèche under light artillery attack to prepare to move off the beach inland to secure a perimeter around the beachhead.

OPPOSITE: A message from the double-agent "Garbo" via Madrid to his German controllers received on 9 June at Hitler's headquaters. He continued to give the impression that the Normandy landings were a diversion before the main invasion by the (non-existent) forces in southeast England.

7 JUNE–25 JULY 1944

BATTLE FOR NORMANDY

The lodgement in Normandy was secure enough by 7 June to prevent a strategic catastrophe, but the progress of the campaign over the following weeks was very much slower than the original plans for "Overlord" had envisaged.

By 11 June, there were 326,000 men ashore supported by 54,000 vehicles; by the middle of the month more than 500,000 men, organized in 19 divisions, had been landed. But even with complete command of the air, Montgomery's forces failed to take the city of Caen, while in the western invasion area Bradley's First US Army finally seized the Cotentin Peninsula and captured the port of Cherbourg after more than three weeks of fighting against comparatively light German resistance.

Montgomery's plan was to force the Germans to concentrate most of their force, including the valuable Panzer divisions, on the front around Caen, so allowing Bradley to break out in the west and swing in a long encirclement behind German armies engaged against the British and Canadians. The operational skills of Rommel's forces combined with the difficult terrain (swampy in places or covered with thick, high hedgerows known as *bocage*) made it difficult for the Allies to bring their advantages to bear. When a fierce gale destroyed one of the floating "mulberry" harbours on 19/20 June, the supply of equipment and men temporarily dried up and Rommel took the opportunity to concentrate his armour for a counter-offensive around Caen which he launched on 1 July. The attack was repulsed in the heaviest fighting since D-Day, but the failure to secure Caen and speed up the collapse of German resistance led to strained relations between Montgomery and a frustrated Eisenhower, who had expected a quick break-out once the lodgement was sufficiently secure and reinforced.

On 7 July, Montgomery began a major operation of his own to seize Caen and break the German line. Following

a massive aerial bombardment, which made progress through the rubble-strewn streets difficult, the town was captured, but Rommel withdrew to a series of five defensive lines constructed to the south, including a concentrated gun line of the formidable "tank-busting" 88-millimetre (3.5-inch) anti-aircraft guns along the Bourguebus Ridge. Urged on by Eisenhower, Montgomery then planned a second operation codenamed "Goodwood" to attack the German defensive zone. The operation was scheduled for 18 July; the day before, Rommel was severely injured when his car was strafed by British aircraft and his command was assumed by Field Marshal von Kluge. On 18 July, the attack began with the heaviest air bombardment of the campaign followed by fierce fighting all through the villages on the Bourguebus Ridge. Torrential rain two days later brought the operation to a halt with the German gun line still intact, but the German command had been forced to move two of the armoured divisions facing Bradley in the west to reinforce the eastern contest. This made it possible for the Americans to break out of Normandy a few days later.

Despite their defensive success, German commanders knew that they could not survive the rate of attrition of German forces. Between D-Day and "Goodwood" they had lost 2,117 tanks and

OPPOSITE: Vehicles drive ashore over the long pontoon bridges of the "mulberry" harbour at Arromanches in August 1944. Before a major port was secured much Allied equipment was shipped through the artificial harbours. The other harbour, at St Laurent, was damaged in a gale in June and could no longer be used, placing even greater strain on Arromanches.

ABOVE: Royal Engineers' blue ensign flown from a "mulberry" harbour pierhead off Arromanches, Normandy.

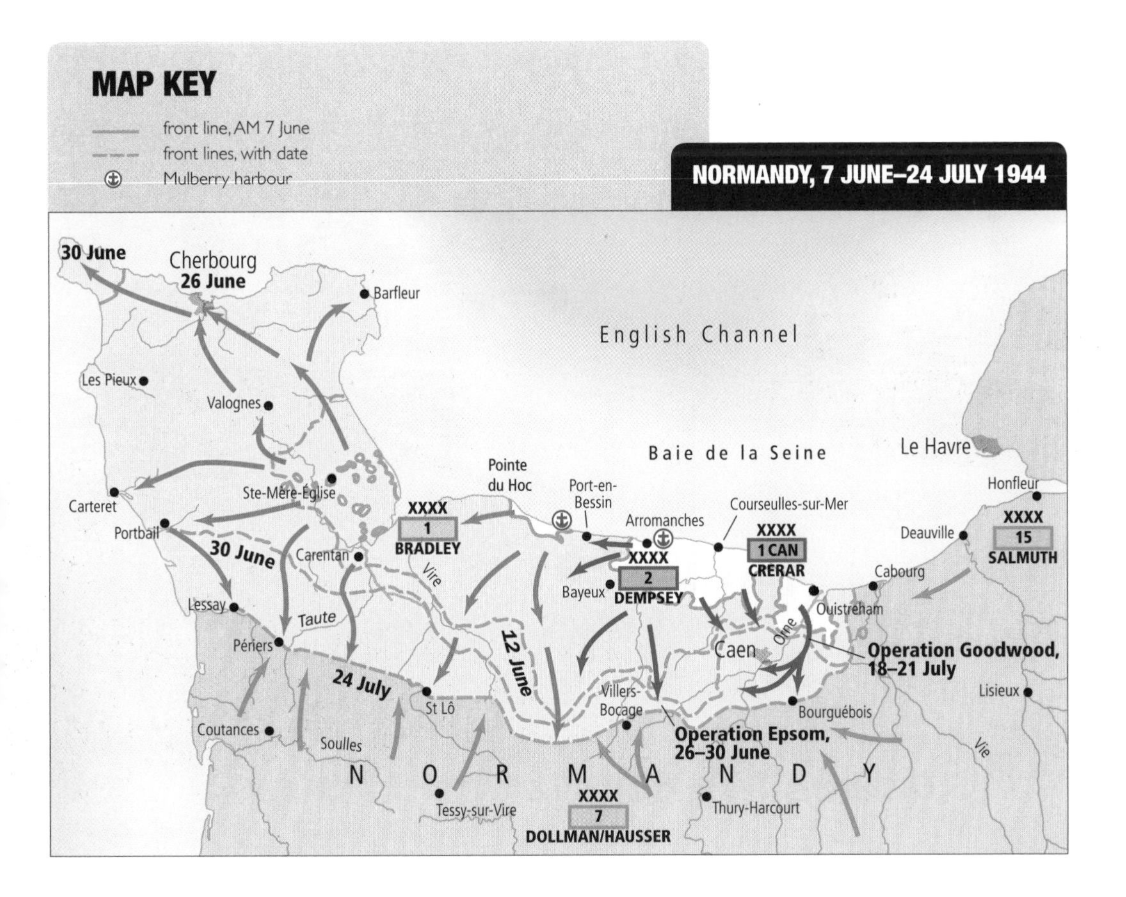

113,000 men and had been sent only 17 tanks and 10,000 men as replacements. Von Kluge wanted to move the front back in an orderly retreat across France, but Hitler insisted that the 7th Army should stand and fight where it was. Allied forces possessed around 4,500 tanks by late July against only 850 German, all but 190 of them facing Montgomery south of Caen. Allied air superiority was overwhelming, around 12,000 aircraft against a total of 1,000 German planes sent to France during June and July, which were shot out of the skies or destroyed at their bases. The defensive circle around the Allies in Normandy was a brittle one by the end of July. Montgomery's strategy had worked sufficiently to create conditions where a final push would produce a German collapse, but it operated too slowly for a supreme commander who wanted quick results. It was Eisenhower's sense of urgency against Montgomery's battlefield prudence that created the postwar myth that the British command failed in Normandy. In reality, the two months of attritional warfare had already broken the back of the German war effort in the West. Within a month almost the whole of France would be in Allied hands.

ABOVE: On 7 July 1944, 467 heavy bombers of the RAF made a devastating attack on the French town of Caen before beginning the operation to capture it from the German 7th Army. Here, on 10 July, a British soldier carries a small girl through the ruins of the city. The rubble made it harder for Allied forces to move through the streets, which were abandoned by the Germans on 9 July.

BELOW: British Cromwell tanks assemble in preparation for the opening of Operation "Goodwood" on 18 July 1944. The operation was designed to break through the German line south of Caen, but poor weather and stiff German defences forced a halt by 20 July.

RIGHT: Part of the diary of Sergeant G E Hughes of the 1st Battalion, Royal Hampshire Regiment, British 50th Division covering the period from D-Day to Operation "Market Garden" in September 1944. He describes the battles around Caen in mid-July 1944 as "Days of Hell".

JUNE 1944

4 Sun—Trinity Sunday

Mass 1000 Hrs
Must be near D DAY
now, roll on lets
get it over with.

5 Mon

D DAY TOMORROW
EVERY BODY QUITE
EXCITED. WE LAND
AT. ~~CAEN~~ Arromanches
Clear 3 Villages & Bayeux

6 Tues—Trinity Law Sittings begin
○ Full Moon

06.00 HRS get in L.C.A. SEA VERY ROUGH ?
HIT THE Beaches at 0720 HRS
murderous fire, losses high I was
lucky T. God, Cleared 3 Villages.
terrible fighting and ghastly sights.

7 Wed Still going dug in at 0200 HRS
away again at 05.30 no FOOD.
writing few notes before we go
into another village. C.O out of
action, adjutant Killed P.Sgt lost
I do P Sgt more later →

JUNE 1944

8 Thur 07.30 fire comeing from
village, Village Cleared
Prisoners taken
Night quite good ~~bed~~
German snipers lurking in wood
had 2 Hrs Sleep ←

9 Fri second rest since the 6th
06.00 Hrs Went on wood
clearing Germans had
flown only one Killed
for our mornings work
we are now about 8 to 10
miles in land 4 armour Div
ahead

10 Sat—s.r. 3.43, s.s. 8.15

Joan Darling I have got
had you all of my thoughts T. God
I have come so far, we have
lost some good men our brigade
was only one to gain full objective
on D DAY.

PROMOTED TO SGT ↑

Mems The french people gave
us a good welcome, had wine
Our casualties high
the landing was
terrible had a near miss

JUNE 1944

18 Sun—2nd after Trinity. Waterloo, 1815

Day of Hell
Counter attack

19 Mon

Day of Hell
Counter attack ?

20 Tues—● New Moon

Day of Hell
advanced, counter
attacked

21 Wed—Longest Day

Quiet Day
we Have been fighting
near Tilley ?
Bayonet Charge
Shelled all day
Letter from Home

JUNE 1944

22 Thur Out on patrol
got within 35 yds of
Tiger before Spotting it
got back safe T. God
Shelled to blazes
Feeling tired out

23 Fri No Sleep last night
exchange of fire, out on
patrols all day
went on O.P for 4 Hrs
stand too all night
Casualties

24 Sat—S. John Baptist
Midsummer Day (Quarter Day)
s.r. 3.43, s.s. 8.21

Up to now all right 1400 Hrs
just had a good dinner
Chicken. Hag to go back
to C.C.S Malaria.

Mems We all expect to
have a leave soon
how true I dont know
Just about had enough
after 19 days.

13 JUNE 1944–29 MARCH 1945

THE V-WEAPONS CAMPAIGN

Under the impact of heavier Allied bombing attacks in 1942 and 1943, Adolf Hitler searched for some new weapon that could be used to attack British cities and perhaps force the Allies to end their bombing campaign.

Two projects appealed particularly to Hitler as weapons of revenge (or *Vergeltungswaffen*): the first was a pilotless flying bomb, the Fieseler-Fi103, developed by the German air force; the second was the first successful ballistic missile, the A-4 rocket, developed by a team of scientists at the research station set up at Peenemünde on the north German coast. The two weapons were known as the V-1 and V-2, the "V" standing for vengeance (*Vergeltung*) in German.

The rocket first flew successfully in October 1942 but there were many technical problems to be overcome with the liquid-fuelled engine and the guidance and control systems. In the summer of 1943, Hitler ordered the manufacture of rockets and flying bombs in tens of thousands but technical difficulties in development, combined with British bombing of the research station on the night of 17/18 August 1943, postponed the introduction of V-weapons until the summer and autumn of 1944. The rockets were taken under the control of Heinrich Himmler's SS construction agency which set up a notorious underground facility at Nordhausen known as Mittelbau Dora; thousands of camp prisoners died in its construction and operation. The Fieseler flying-bomb was easier to produce and it came into operation in the summer of 1944 when, on 13 June, the first bombs were launched against London.

British intelligence had already identified the potential threat of new weapons and from December 1943 bomber forces based in Britain were ordered to attack the weapons' production facilities and launch sites in an operation

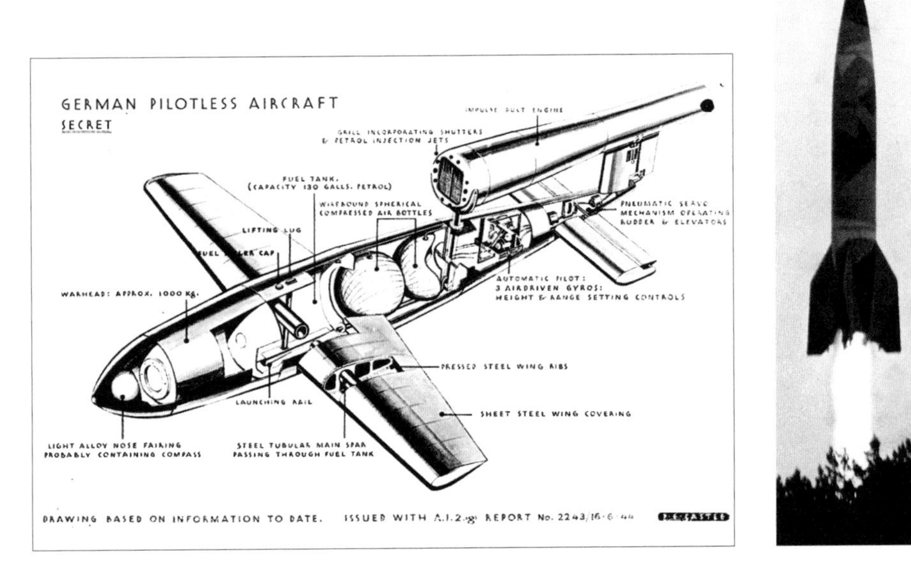

RIGHT: A cut-away drawing of of the V-1 Weapon, the Fiesler-Fi103 pilotless missile. It was first tested in December 1942, and around 10,000 of the missiles were launched against southern England causing widespread destruction.

FAR RIGHT: The test launch of a V-2 weapon, the A-4 rocket, from the SS troop training area near Cracow in Poland in 1944. The weapons were large and complex pieces of engineering but carried a warhead of just over 900 kilogrammes (2,000 pounds) in weight, a fraction of the payload carried by a single Allied bomber. However, the rocket's high speed gave the warhead added impact when it struck the ground.

codenamed "Crossbow". The campaign reached its height during the period June to September 1944, when 60,000 tons of bombs were dropped on V-1 targets. "Crossbow" succeeded in disrupting the V-weapons programme but not in halting it. Over 10,000 flying bombs were directed at London and a number of other British cities, but only 7,488 reached England and of these only 2,419 reached London. The death toll of 6,184 was nevertheless high in proportion to the tonnage of explosive and a more effective flying-bomb campaign might well have provoked a crisis in the capital. From October 1944 the V-1 was also directed at the Belgian port of Antwerp, which was a major supply base for Allied armies.

A high proportion of V-1s were shot down by aircraft or anti-aircraft fire before they reached their target, while misinformation fed from double-agents in Britain led the Germans to believe that their missiles were going too far north. The trajectory was readjusted and as a result many fell short of London on rural areas of the southeast.

Against the A-4 rocket there was less security. The first missile was fired on 8 September 1944. It was by its nature an imprecise weapon and the 517 rockets that hit London did so in no predictable pattern, causing the deaths of a further 2,754 civilians. The rocket was fired from small easily-concealed silos and was difficult to attack from the air. Once in flight only technical malfunction would prevent its arrival at its destination. Of the 6,000 V-2s produced, only 1,054 rockets hit England between 8 September and 27 March 1945; a further 900 were directed at Antwerp in the last months of 1944. Hitler's plan to produce the weapons in tens of thousands was frustrated by the collapse of the German war economy, fatally damaged by the impact of Allied heavy bombing.

As well as the V-1 and V-2, other weapons were developed, but they failed to see service. The V-3 long-range gun, designed to fire special shells a distance of almost 160 kilometres (100 miles), was developed in 1943 and 1944 but had to be abandoned when bombers hit the two designated sites near Calais in November 1943 and July 1944. A further weapon, the so-called V-4, was a ground-to-air missile codenamed "Wasserfall" (waterfall) which was close to mass-production in 1944 but lacked the support of Hitler in the struggle for scarce resources. The ground-to-air rocket might well have played a vital role in the war against Allied bombers but the V-1 and V-2 did nothing to dent the combined bomber offensive.

OPPOSITE: A group of V-1 weapons at a launch site somewhere in France. The wings were folded back during transport and the weapon prepared at the launching area before being fired from a small inclined launch ramp.

LEFT: A British policeman comforts a survivor of a V-1 attack near Gipsy Hill in London in 1944. The missile destroyed a street of houses, killing the man's wife and wrecking his house. Almost 9,000 people were killed in the V-weapons campaign.

MARCH–SEPTEMBER 1944

DEFEAT OF THE LUFTWAFFE

At the start of the Second World War, the German air force was second in size only to the Soviet air force, and was the most advanced in terms of the quality of equipment and the training of its pilots.

The air force played an important part in securing the rapid victories in 1939–41, and, though smaller in size, it destroyed the Soviet air force on the ground and in the air during the opening stages of "Barbarossa". By 1944, however, the force faced serious crisis and during the course of the year was effectively defeated, contributing

OPPOSITE BELOW:
A squadron of German Messerschmitt Bf 110 night-fighters flying over Germany in the summer of 1944. Because of its heavy armament of guns and rockets, the Bf 110 could inflict heavy damage on Allied bombers. By day they were easy prey for the long-range Allied fighters.

RIGHT:
Long-range fuel tanks being fitted on an RAF Hawker Typhoon Mark IB fighter-bomber to enable it to carry out strikes on distant targets in Germany. The introduction of extra fuel capacity transformed the air war over Germany in a matter of months.

to the collapse of German resistance on all fronts in the last year of the war.

The major problem facing the German air force was the impact of the Combined Bomber Offensive, launched by the British and US bomber forces from the spring of 1943. The bombing by day and by night forced the German air force to keep more and more of its fighter aircraft in Germany to defend the home economy and population, and to distort German aircraft production in favour of fighters rather than bombers and dive-bombers. In January 1943, 59 per cent of the fighter force was in the Reich, by January 1944 68 per cent, and by September 1944 some 80 per cent. By 1944 bomber output, so essential for the support of the front-line campaigns, constituted only one-fifth of German aircraft production, as compared to over half at the start of the war. The decline in the numbers of aircraft at the fighting fronts meant a high level of attrition against more heavily armed opponents. On D-Day, only 170 German aircraft were available in northwest France against the 12,000 aircraft of the Western Allies. Air superiority passed to the Allies in France, in Italy and on the Eastern Front.

Bombing also disrupted the production of aircraft, aero-engines and components. Germany was outproduced in aircraft by each of its major adversaries over the course of the war. In 1944, against the 39,807 aircraft produced in Germany and the satellite territories, the Allies produced 163,079. In 1944, the Combined Bomber Offensive was directed at German aircraft output and oil production in order to undermine the efforts still being made to combat Allied bombing. For six days, starting on 20 February, bomber forces launched Operation "Argument", better known as "Big Week", against the German aircraft industry. Altogether RAF Bomber Command and the US Eighth Air Force dropped 20,000 tons of bombs on air production targets. This did not destroy production, but forced an improvised dispersal and held back the expansion of German output. More damaging was the attack on oil installations during 1944, which reduced the supply of oil by September to 31 per cent of what it had been in January, while the output of aviation fuel was temporarily reduced to just five per cent of requirements. The lack of oil made it difficult to train pilots, and contributed to the high loss rates of German aviators during 1944.

The most important factor was the Anglo-American development, late in 1943, of an effective long-range fighter to contest German air space. The P-51 Mustang fighter began as a design produced for the British using a Rolls Royce Merlin engine, but even loaded with extra fuel tanks, its fighting capacity was little impaired. It was chosen to accompany Eighth Air Force bombers and in December 1943 made its first fighting appearance over the German port of Kiel. In March 1944, Mustangs flew 2,900 kilometres (1,800 miles) to Berlin and back. A crash production programme was pushed through and during the spring and summer of 1944 the Mustang, together with other fighters converted to operate at long-range, contested German air space for the first time. The attrition rate for the German fighter force increased sharply, from around 20 per cent losses per month late in 1943 to more than 50 per cent every month in the spring and summer of 1944. Although German production rose to more than 3,000 fighters a month, they were destroyed piecemeal at the factories, at their bases or in the air, flown by pilots who had been trained for much of the time on simulators for lack of fuel. During 1944, the RAF resumed occasional daylight bombing because the risk from German fighters was so reduced. Not even the development of the first jet fighter, the Messerschmitt Me 262, could reverse the outcome, because far too few were available. The massive bombing attacks of the last year of war on the German homeland were made possible by the neutralization of the Luftwaffe.

5 JUNE–31 DECEMBER 1944

STALEMATE IN ITALY

When the allied Army entered Rome on 4 June 1944 there was hope that the campaign in Italy might now be decided by the autumn.

German forces under Field Marshal Kesselring, together with a small number of Italian Fascist forces still loyal to Mussolini, pulled rapidly northwards, towards other prepared lines of defence. What followed was a long and gruelling campaign that did not see Allied victory until the very end of the war in Europe, in May 1945.

The decision to divert forces to Rome opened up a gap between American and British armies and allowed the German army to extricate itself from a potential trap. No real effort was made to pursue the retreating enemy, and Kesselring was able to draw his forces north to the Arno Line running through Pisa and Florence to the Adriatic coast. Behind this line was the more heavily defended Gothic Line, running from just south of La Spezia through the Apennine Mountains to the coast at Pesaro. Allied forces in Italy under General Alexander followed the Germans to the Arno river, all but one of whose bridges had been blown up, but Kesselring declined to fight for the Arno Line. Livorno was captured on 19 July, Florence on 13 August. By mid-August, both the British 8th Army and the US Fifth Army were approaching the Gothic Line.

The 8th Army commander, Lieutenant General Oliver Leese, persuaded Alexander to allow him to launch Operation "Olive" to break the Gothic Line along the Adriatic coast where it was thought that armour could deploy more easily. The loss of six divisions for the invasion of southern France forced a temporary halt in preparations. The 8th Army attacked on 25 August and, despite the difficulty of crossing the rivers along the coast, was by 4 September fighting for the coastal town of Rimini, which fell on 21 September. Kesselring moved his reserves to blunt the British attack and against the now weakened centre the US Second Corps attacked towards Bologna, breaching the Gothic Line again. German reserves were moved again

and poor weather together with determined German defence halted General Clark's attack only 14 kilometres (nine miles) from Bologna, while the 8th Army, facing heavy rain and poor terrain, moved slowly towards Ravenna, which was reached in December.

The German 10th and 14th armies held what was now called the Genghis Khan Line from Bologna to Argenta on the east coast. The Allied attack faltered and in an exceptionally bad winter a stalemate descended over the front. For the Germans and their remaining Italian Fascist allies this was the opportunity to deal with the threat posed by an estimated 82,000 Italian partisans in the German-occupied north who had already embarked on a major confrontation with the German army as the Allies moved north. Around six of the 26 German divisions were forced to combat the Italian resistance. In northwestern Italy the Alpine passes had been freed from Axis control and small areas of partisan rule established.

The end of the Allied advance allowed the Germans to turn their full attention against the partisans, even more so when Alexander had it broadcast on the radio on 13 November that the Allies would stay where they were for the winter, advising the partisans to stop fighting and await further orders. The result was disastrous. The Voluntary Freedom Corps under General Raffaele Cadorna, which co-ordinated partisan operations, found itself subject to large sweeping operations by German forces and two Cossack cavalry divisions fighting for the Axis. The anti-partisan campaign was conducted with extraordinary brutality against the civil population, and much of the area controlled by the partisans was seized back again. By the end of the campaign the resistance was down to around 20,000 men and women, reviving again only later in 1945 when the Allied advance began once again. Around 40,000 partisans perished in the fighting.

OPPOSITE: Italian civilians pick their way through the rubble of the Ponte all Grazie over the Arno river in Florence in August 1944, returning to the northern part of the city after the German evacuation on 11 August. The only bridge not destroyed was the Ponte Vecchio.

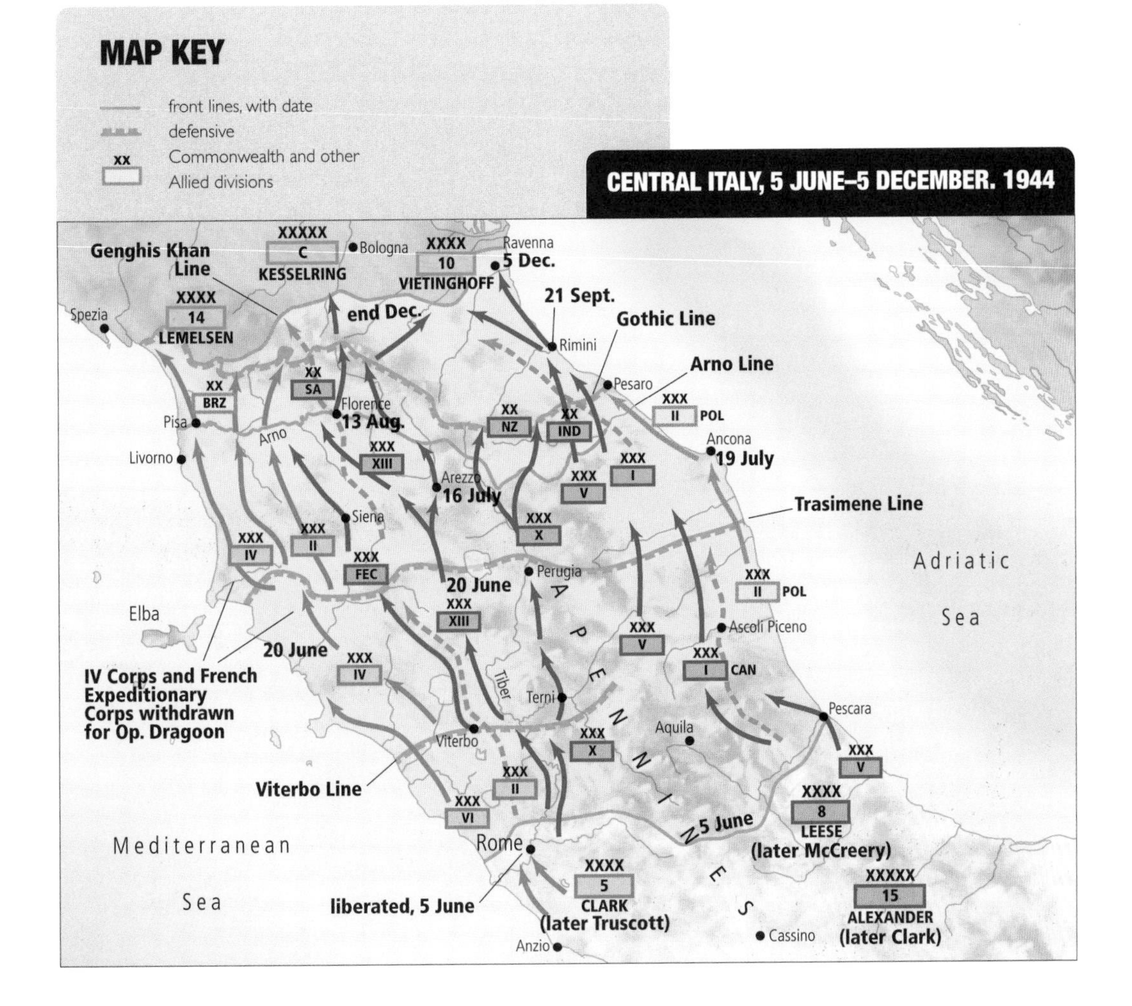

1939–1945

BEHIND BARBED WIRE: THE FATE OF POWS

Of the many millions of men and women mobilized to fight the Second World War, a substantial proportion became prisoners of the enemy.

Their treatment and survival rates varied a great deal between the different combatant powers. In many cases, in contravention of the Geneva Convention, they were used as forced labour for war-related purposes. In some cases, most notably the German efforts to recruit a Russian Liberation Army from captured Red Army soldiers, prisoners became soldiers fighting against their former comrades.

The number of prisoners caught reflected the pattern of victory or defeat. Around 5.2 million Soviet soldiers were captured in the period of German victories in the east, when great encirclement operations ensnared whole Soviet armies. From 1944, it was the turn of the Soviet side to capture large numbers of Germans, while Soviet POW losses declined sharply. The British captured 600,000 Italian (including Italian colonial) soldiers in Africa, many of whom had no stomach for the contest; in Sicily, too, Italian soldiers surrendered in large numbers. German soldiers were captured in millions only in the last weeks of the war when American, British Commonwealth and French forces defeated the German army in Germany and Italy. In the Asian and Pacific wars, Japan took large numbers of prisoners in the first weeks of the war in 1941–42, but thereafter relatively few; Japanese soldiers were ordered

OPPOSITE: A view of the German POW camp for air force prisoners Stalag Luft III, at Sagan in Silesia, Germany, 1944. This camp was the site of a major escape attempt, which was later made famous by the film *The Great Escape*.

RIGHT: Italian POWs load sacks of sugar destined for liberated Europe at Falcon Spinning Mill, Bolton, Lancashire in March 1945. Although Italy was now one of the Allied co-belligerent states, many Italian POWs continued to work for the Allies until after the end of the war.

not to surrender, and around 1.7 million Japanese soldiers, sailors and airmen died in the war, fighting suicidally rather than give in.

Once captured, the fate of prisoners was highly variable. In the war in the West both sides respected as far as they could the 1929 Geneva Convention (though on both sides there were cases where prisoners were killed on the battlefield) and camps were visited by the Red Cross. In most camps, the NCOs were responsible for keeping the discipline of their own rank and file, which in the case of some POW camps for SS soldiers in Britain led to kangaroo courts and the murder of anti-Hitler Germans. For servicemen caught in the West, there was an endless round of camp sports, entertainment, camp newspapers and journals and occasional attempts at escape. Since many Axis prisoners were sent to the United States, Canada and Australia, escape was pointless. But British and American servicemen regularly tried to escape from German prison camps and, once free, to contact underground escape organizations which could help them reach Switzerland, Sweden, Spain or Portugal. Around 35,000 escaped or evaded capture during the war. In Britain, prisoners were recruited to work on farms and building projects, and after the war, German POWs were kept back from repatriation

COLDITZ CASTLE

The eleventh-century German castle at Colditz, in Saxony, was used during the Second World War as a prison camp for officers who were either inveterate escapers or regarded as a security risk. The castle had been used as a mental asylum between 1829 and 1924, and during the early years of the Third Reich housed political prisoners and so-called "asocials". In 1939, designated Oflag IV-C, it became a camp for Polish and French officers, then a high-security camp for escapers, including Wing Commander Douglas Bader. The nature of the prison population made further escape attempts inevitable. There were around 300 attempts, and 30 successful escapes. The war ended before a glider, under construction in an attic area, could be used to mount yet another escape bid.

until 1947–48, despite protests, because they provided a necessary contribution to British economic recovery.

On the Eastern Front, the prisoner regime was much harsher. Neither Germany nor the Soviet Union had been prepared for the scale of the prisoner population. Red Army soldiers were herded into makeshift enclosures in the summer and autumn of 1941 and typhus became endemic. Lack of food, shelter and sanitation decimated the prisoner population and an estimated 2.4 to 3 million died. Eventually, in response to labour shortages in Germany, Hitler agreed to allow Soviet prisoners to be transported west to work, predominantly on essential military building projects and in agriculture.

Prisoners of the Japanese were also forced to work, usually in debilitating conditions and subject to savage punishments, inflicted in part because the Japanese despised soldiers who surrendered or were captured. Captured Chinese soldiers were often murdered, and occasionally recruited to fight for the local Japanese militia.

Many POWs continued to suffer once the war was over. German soldiers died in the makeshift camps set up by the Western Allies, who had simply nowhere to house them and no plan to supply them with food. Red Army prisoners returned to the Soviet Union were all interrogated by SMERSH, the anti-spying organization set up in 1943, and many were sent to labour camps from fear that they had been contaminated by fascism. For prisoners free to return home there were ambiguous feelings provoked both by defeat and also by victory in which they had been unable to take part.

OPPOSITE Frederick J Want of Cromfield Road Stratford, London and Charles Freeman of Kings Road Middlesbrough, after they had suffered 3½ years of Japanese starvation.

RIGHT German POWs working in the vegetable garden at Glen Mill POW camp in Oldham, Lancashire on Christmas Eve 1940. Few German prisoners had yet been captured and not until 1942 were significant numbers in British hands.

17–26 SEPTEMBER 1944

OPERATION "MARKET GARDEN"

The sudden collapse of German resistance in France in August 1944 opened up the prospect that the war in the West might be brought to a rapid conclusion if Allied armies could penetrate into Germany fast enough.

Montgomery's 21st Army Group and Bradley's Twelfth Army Group pushed on into eastern France and Belgium during September. On 4 September, the port of Antwerp was captured, but not the Scheldt estuary to the north, which was still defended by scattered German units, making it impossible to use the major port for supplying Allied armies. The sheer

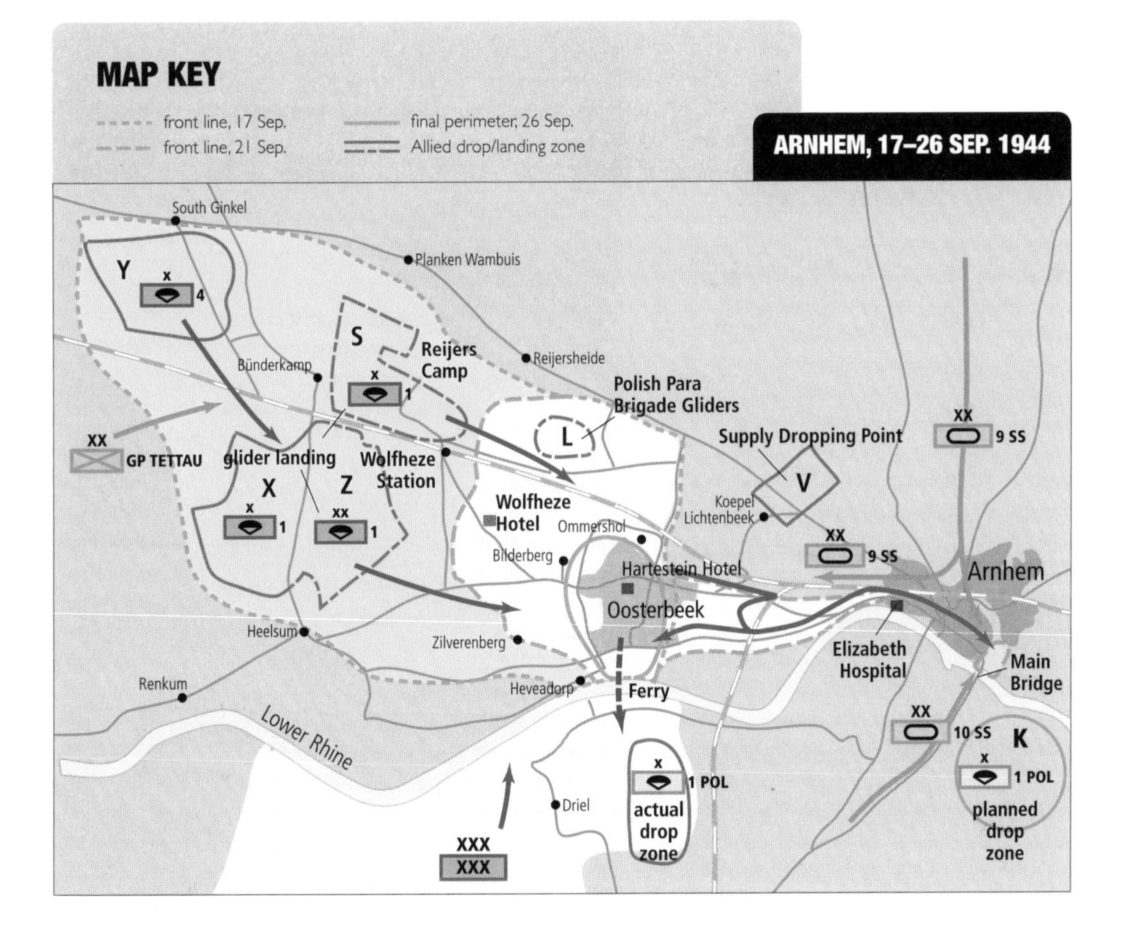

speed of the advance had produced a crisis of supply which threatened to undermine the ambition to destroy German resistance by the winter.

It was in this strategic context that Montgomery now suggested a daring operation to try to accelerate the Allied advance. "Market Garden" was designed to drive a salient into the German line towards the Dutch city of Arnhem, force a crossing of the lower Rhine and create the conditions for Allied forces to sweep down towards the industrial region of the Ruhr. It was an ambitious plan, and left the estuary around Antwerp still in enemy hands, but on 10 September Eisenhower approved it and agreed to make available the First Allied Airborne Army led by US Lieutenant General Lewis Brereton, but under the tactical command of the British Lieutenant General Frederick Browning. The three airborne divisions were allocated different tasks. The US 82nd and 101st Divisions were to seize the Nijmegen and Eindhoven bridges over the River Waal and the Wilhelmina canal, while the British 1st Airborne Division was to capture the bridges at Arnhem and create a narrow bridgehead across the Rhine. While the airborne forces fought for the bridges, Lieutenant General Horrocks was to bring his 30th Corps forward through the narrow passageway carved out of the German line to strengthen the Allied grip on Arnhem.

The operation began on 17 September with mixed fortunes. The 19,000 troops were dropped into the combat zones more accurately than was often the case, but the attempt to cross eight water barriers was in itself a challenge. Browning insisted on taking part in the operation personally, taking the whole headquarters staff by glider to Arnhem, but he found it difficult to hold together the scattered airborne units with poor radio communications. The American divisions succeeded in taking their objectives in Eindhoven and Nijmegen, but further north the 1st Airborne Division met stiff German resistance and failed to take the bridges over the Rhine. The 9th and 10th SS Panzer Divisions were refitting at Arnhem and although Browning had been warned by his intelligence officers that the divisions had been detected, he chose to launch the operation regardless. The

OPPOSITE: An aerial view of Airspeed Horsa and GAL Hamilcar gliders on Landing Zone "Z" near Wolfheze woods, northwest of the Dutch city of Arnhem on 17 September 1944. Operation "Market Garden" depended on the successful transport of airborne forces and equipment, including the operation's headquarters staff and commander.

result was strong German counter-attacks in and around Arnhem that forced the British 2nd Parachute Battalion to surrender on 21 September. The expected help from the 30th Corps did not materialize. Horrocks's units were held up by the slow process of bridge-building and by bad weather and reached the River Waal only on 21 September. They crossed it the following day, only to find that the British position was now hopeless. Airborne forces were ordered to make their way back across the Waal on 25 September and the operation was abandoned.

Montgomery's gamble failed to pay off and involved a heavy cost. The 1st Airborne Division suffered 7,842 casualties, including 6,000 prisoners. The two American divisions, which held the salient they had formed for a further two months, suffered total casualties of 3,532. Browning took much of the blame for the failure, but he had famously warned Montgomery early in September that Arnhem might be "a bridge too far". In October and November 1944, Montgomery concentrated instead on clearing the Scheldt estuary and freeing Antwerp as a supply base, a campaign that was only completed on 8 November with the capture of Walcheren at the mouth of the river. By late November, the port could at last be used, but Allied armies had been brought to a halt along the German frontier where months of bitter fighting still lay ahead.

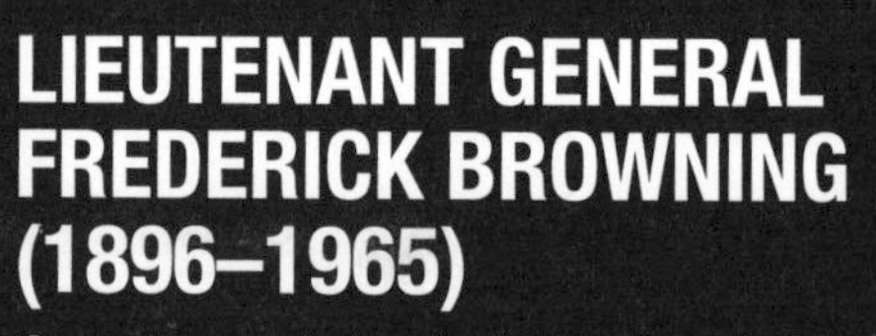

LIEUTENANT GENERAL FREDERICK BROWNING (1896–1965)

Generally regarded as the father of the British airborne forces, Frederick Browning began his career in the First World War with the Grenadier Guards. He was a Guards commander in the early years of the Second World War until appointed in October 1941 to command the British 1st Airborne Division. He designed the distinctive maroon beret for the force and played a key part in their organization and training. In April 1943, he became airborne advisor to Eisenhower in the Mediterranean theatre where he helped to plan the Sicily invasion, and in December 1943 was commander of Headquarters Airborne Troops under Montgomery. After the Normandy invasion, he became deputy commander of the 1st Allied Airborne Army and in this capacity helped to organize and lead Operation "Market Garden". After its failure he was sent as chief-of-staff to the Southeast Asia Command. After the war, he became comptroller of the Royal Household.

BELOW LEFT: A Lloyd carrier of the anti-tank platoon of the 3rd Battalion, Irish Guards explodes on the road towards Eindhoven as the British 30th Corps begins its advance to meet up with forces in Arnhem on 17 September 1944.

BELOW RIGHT: A German infantry battalion hunting for British troops in the suburbs of Arnhem during the battle for the river crossings in the town. German resistance was heavier than anticipated.

ABOVE: A line of British paratroopers captured by the German defenders of Arnhem. After months of Allied success in Western Europe, Arnhem was a sharp reminder of the remaining fighting-power of the German enemy. Around 6,000 Allied soldiers were taken prisoner.

RIGHT: Four British paratroopers move cautiously through a ruined house in Oosterbeek where they had been forced to retreat after abandoning Arnhem. The picture was taken on 23 September 1944 by a photographer of the Army Film and Photographic Unit sent to accompany the 1st Allied Airborne Army during the operation.

LIEUTENANT GENERAL BRIAN HORROCKS (1895–1985)

Brian Horrocks was one of the most popular and well-regarded British generals of the Second World War whose long army career was spiced with incident. He almost failed his cadet course at Sandhurst, but the outbreak of the First World War gave him the opportunity to prove himself in battle. He was wounded and captured in October 1914 and spent four years trying to escape; in exasperation the Germans put him in a Russian POW camp, where he learnt fluent Russian. On repatriation in 1919 he volunteered to serve with the British intervention in Russia where he was captured again in January 1920 and held as a prisoner for 10 months. He had become a career soldier and by the outbreak of war was an instructor at the staff college. He commanded a machine-gun battalion in France, and a division in Britain in 1941. He was sent to North Africa to command the 13th Corps under Montgomery in 1942, where his unit defended the Alam Halfa ridge in the battle in early September 1942. He played a key role in Tunisia and accepted the surrender of Rommel's Afrika Korps. In June 1943 he was severely wounded, but in August 1944 was back in command of 30th Corps which he led in Operation "Market Garden". At the end of the war he was promoted to lieutenant general and in 1949 he was appointed gentleman usher of the Black Rod in the House of Lords.

7 MARCH–25 APRIL 1945

THE WESTERN ADVANCE INTO GERMANY: FROM THE RHINE TO THE ELBE

At the end of 1944, the Western Allies were poised to begin the assault on Germany when the Battle of the Bulge interrupted their preparations.

The effect was not entirely negative, for the final fling of German forces in the west removed the last major reserves of tanks and aircraft and left the three German army groups – General Student's Group H in the north in the Netherlands, Group B under Field Marshal Model in the Ruhr and Group G under General Blaskowitz in the south – well under strength and devoid of serious air support.

Eisenhower favoured an approach on a broad front, as the Red Army was doing in the east. By 3 January, he had 73 divisions, 20 of them armoured and the rest well-equipped, supported by overwhelming strength in the air, both tactical and strategic. The campaign to bring the war to an end involved three stages: clearing the territory on the west bank of the Rhine, effecting a series of Rhine crossings to establish solid bridgeheads on the eastern bank, and finally a general break-out to bring Western armies to the River Elbe and into Austria and Czechoslovakia, where they would meet up with the Soviet armed forces. Although Montgomery would have preferred a breakthrough on a narrower front and rapid deployment towards Berlin, Eisenhower accepted the decision agreed at Yalta that Berlin would be in the Soviet zone of operations.

The first series of operations was launched on 8 February 1945 when Montgomery's Twenty-first Army Group, under the codename "Veritable", began an attack to clear the area between the River Meuse and the Rhine. The British 2nd Army and Canadian 1st Army encountered fierce resistance from the German 1st Paratroop Army in the Reichswald forest and not until 21 February was the northern area west of the Rhine cleared. The US Ninth Army, mounting Operation "Grenade", was held up by flooding and could only begin on 23 February, but weak German resistance brought them to the bank of the Rhine near Düsseldorf on 1 March. Further south, Bradley's Twelfth Army Group, in Operation "Lumberjack", cut rapidly through the defences of the Westwall, the main frontier fortifications, to reach the river by 7 March, while Operation "Undertone", led by Lieutenant General Jacob Devers's Sixth Army Group, pushed forward into the Saarland to reach Mannheim on the southern Rhine.

It was during the "Lumberjack" operation that the US Ninth Armored Division surprised German troops trying to demolish the Hindenburg railway bridge over the river at Remagen. They captured the bridge intact on 7 March and established a small bridgehead on the far side. Despite efforts to destroy the bridge with V-2 rockets, it survived until 17 March, when it finally collapsed. Eisenhower insisted on maintaining a broad front nevertheless, and Montgomery planned a massive assault across the river between Rees and Duisburg. German forces had been reduced to a mere 26 divisions, by contrast with more than 200 facing the Red Army in the east. To cope with the expected assault, Hitler replaced the faithful von Rundstedt with Field Marshal Kesselring, the defender of Italy. There were simply too few soldiers and too little equipment to hold up the assault for long. When the Rhine was crossed in force on 24 March in the north a broad bridgehead was easily secured. Ever mindful of the opportunity to get the better of the British, General Patton made his crossing further south at Oppenheim two days before, on the night of 22/23 March.

Unequal though the contest was, it would be wrong to see it as a straightforward campaign. German forces often fought with fanatical determination and great tactical skill and high casualties were exacted in the last month of the conflict, but the final outcome was not in doubt. On 1 April, Model's forces were trapped in the area of the Ruhr, and on 21 April the encircled German armies surrendered, an

estimated 350,000 men in total. Meanwhile, Montgomery's Twenty-first Army Group reached the ruins of Lübeck on the Baltic coast. Further south, resistance crumbled. The US Ninth Army reached Magdeburg on the Elbe river on 12 April, while forward units of Lieutenant General Hodges's US First Army reached the Elbe on 25 April near the town of Torgau where they experienced a historic meeting with units of Konev's 1st Ukrainian Army Group. The US Sixth Army Group, which included the French 1st Army under General de Lattre de Tassigny, cleared southern Germany and moved into Austria. It was now only a matter of time before Germany was utterly defeated.

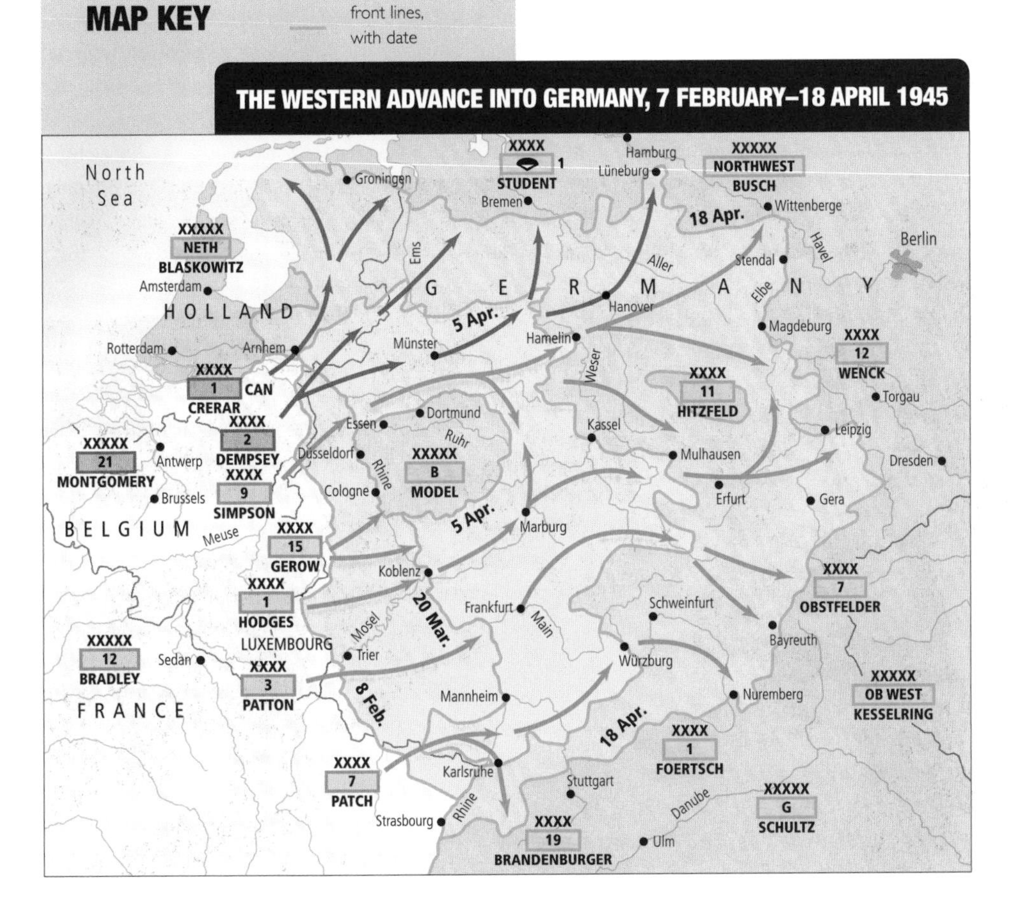

OPPOSITE: British troops of the Gordon Highlanders fighting in the Reichswald forest in northwest Germany, 9 February 1945. Fighting here was fierce against five defensive lines and in heavy mud. The forest was finally cleared by 9 March.

ABOVE: Winston Churchill lunching with Field Marshal Montgomery and Field Marshal Alan Brooke, chief of the Imperial General Staff, on the east bank of the Rhine on 26 March 1945, two days after the British assault across the river.

JULY 1944–MAY 1945

LIBERATION OF THE CAMPS

When the Allies finally advanced towards the German homeland, they began to uncover clear evidence of the atrocious nature of the regime Hitler's Germany had imposed on political prisoners, on so-called "asocials" (vagrants, the workshy, homosexuals, recidivist criminals etc.), on Gypsies and above all on the Jews of Europe.

These many groups had been transported to one of a number of different kinds of camp. By 1944, there were 20 major concentration camps, with 165 sub-camps. Here prisoners were expected to work in difficult conditions. The death rate was exceptionally high, from disease and malnutrition as much as deliberate murder, but the object was to make the prisoners labour. There were also seven main extermination camps – where Jews and other prisoners were sent for immediate murder in purpose-built centres with gas chambers and crematoria – at Majdanek, Sobibor, Chelmno, Belzec, Treblinka, Auschwitz-Birkenau (by far the largest) and a smaller facility at Maly Trostenets. At least 3.5 million people died in these camps. Majdanek and Auschwitz also served as concentration camps.

OPPOSITE: Some of the female prisoners at Auschwitz shortly after their liberation by the Red Army in late January 1945. Mainly the sick or disabled remained after thousands of other prisoners were marched westwards to other camps. Soviet inmates were then interrogated by Soviet counter-intelligence in the buildings of the camp.

RIGHT: On 24 April 1945, nine days after the camp was liberated, a British army chaplain holds a brief service over a mass grave in the German concentration camp of Bergen-Belsen before it is covered over.

These two, Auschwitz and Majdanek, were the first major camps to be liberated, both uncovered by the Red Army as it marched through Poland. In Majdanek in July 1944, the Red Army found 1,000 emaciated prisoners and warehouses full of hair, cases, clothing and children's toys. Auschwitz-Birkenau, half slave camp, half extermination centre, was occupied on 27 January 1945 after many of the prisoners had been forced to leave on foot 10 days earlier on one of the many "death marches" of the last months of war. Here the Soviet soldiers found around 3,000 prisoners in the main camp, many close to death. They also found more evidence of German scrupulousness – stores of 380,000 men's suits and 836,000 women's coats and dresses, and 7.7 tons of human hair, packed and ready to transport. But the other evidence of mass killings had been destroyed and the crematoria ovens blown up. The true horror of the camp was revealed by Soviet prisoners found there, who were interrogated by SMERSH, the military security organization, in the same buildings where they had been prisoners shortly before. The Soviet authorities had allowed some visits to Majdanek by foreign representatives, but the liberation of Auschwitz was not announced until 7 May, after the German surrender.

In the West, no extermination camps were uncovered, for these had been built on occupied Polish or Belorussian territory. British Commonwealth and American forces came across concentration camps instead, where by April 1945 conditions were lethal in the extreme. Lack of food, the absence of any form of hygiene or effective medical care, coupled with the growing brutality of the guards as the war drew to a close, created conditions in which huge numbers of prisoners died. As the German boundaries contracted, thousands of prisoners were marched from overrun camps to the few that remained in operation. It was this final migration of prisoners that caused the terrible scenes found by the British 8th Corps when units entered the camp at Bergen-Belsen in northwestern Germany on 15 April 1945. The camp had held 15,000 prisoners in December 1944, but by April there were between 40,000 and 50,000, many of them Jews forced to march on foot to the camp from sites further east. The piles of corpses and the hollow-eyed, starving prisoners became the standard images of German atrocity and were sent to newspapers in the West immediately after liberation.

The prisoners in Bergen-Belsen, where the camp was infected with typhus, continued to die in large numbers after liberation. In the end 14,000 of the 40,000 prisoners died. German civilians from the locality were brought in to view the camp on 24 April 1945, and it was burned down on British army orders in June. Further south, the American army liberated Dachau camp on 29 April. As a unit of the US 45th Division approached the camp, they found 39 rail cars filled with dead and decomposing bodies. As the soldiers approached the camp, SS guards opened fire. They were rushed by the prisoners and beaten to death. Around 70,000 prisoners were found in the Dachau system. The liberation of the camps provoked horror and outrage among the troops that first arrived on the scene, but in many cases it took years before the perpetrators were finally brought to trial.

JANUARY 1945–28 AUGUST 1945

VICTORY IN BURMA

After the failure of the Japanese offensive in northern India against Imphal and Kohima, Lieutenant General Slim's 14th Army began to plan the reconquest of Burma.

Allied forces moved forward to the Chindwin River in western Burma, while in the north a combination of Indian forces and General Stilwell's Chinese divisions cleared the last Japanese forces and finally opened the Ledo Road (renamed at Chiang Kaishek's suggestion the Stilwell Road) in January 1945 to transport supplies to the Chinese army facing the Japanese in southern China.

Slim's plan, codenamed Operation "Capital", followed by "Extended Capital", was to drive across the Chindwin into the central Shwebo Plain, across the River Irrawaddy and on to the Burmese capital of Rangoon (Yangon). This operation involved first capturing Akyab on the coast of the Bay of Bengal, which could be used as an air base. A mixed British-Indian force captured the town on 4 January and moved on down the coast, driving the Japanese 28th Army towards the Arakan Mountains. In the central plain, Slim's forces captured Shwebo by 8 January, but then faced growing Japanese resistance from the Japanese 33rd Army stationed to defend Mandalay and the path to the south.

Slim undertook an elaborate deception plan which involved persuading the Japanese command in Burma, under Lieutenant General Hyotaro Kimura, that Mandalay

FAR LEFT: Indians of the 6/7 Rajput Rifles mop up remaining Japanese resistance in Pyawbwe, north of Rangoon on 11 April 1945. The Burmese capital was occupied by 5 May as the Japanese army withdrew eastwards.

LEFT: The Burma Star, awarded to those who served in the Burma campaign between December 1941 and September 1945.

was the main objective for the northern Allied force, while the rest of 4th Corps went south through the mountains to outflank the Japanese and cross the Irrawaddy at Pakokku. The strategy worked almost perfectly. Against light resistance, the British and Indian forces crossed the river further south and drove for the communications centre at Meiktilan where a fierce battle took place against the Japanese 15th Army commanded by Lieutenant General Shihachi Katamura. The Japanese were caught between two forces and were not strong enough to contain both. Mandalay fell on 20 March to the northern forces, while positions around Meiktila, briefly surrounded and besieged by the Japanese, were abandoned on 29 March. There was now little between Slim's force and the city of Rangoon further to the south.

Two separate attacks were made towards the capital, one led by Lieutenant General Stopford down the Irrawaddy valley, the other by Lieutenant General Messervy along the Sittang river. His flank was protected by the Burma Independence Army of Aung San, which changed sides in March to help end Japanese domination in Burma. Slim was anxious that Rangoon should be captured before the onset of the monsoon rains in May, and to be certain of it he organized a further operation, for the 26th Indian Division on the Arakan Coast to be taken by ship to the coast below Rangoon to take it from the sea. When the division arrived on 3 May, the Japanese had already abandoned the struggle and retreated east across the Sittang river. The forces from the north met up with the southern invasion force on 5 May and the whole of central Burma was in Allied hands.

The Japanese army was never defeated entirely in Burma. The 28th Army in the hills of Arakan tried in July 1945 to break out eastwards from its encirclement. Forewarned by intelligence sources, the British Commonwealth forces imposed 17,000 casualties at the cost of only 95 of their own. Intermittent fighting continued along the Sittang river until on 28 August the Japanese surrendered formally in Rangoon. The whole operation to reconquer Burma cost only 3,188 Allied dead; Japanese dead totalled 23,000. Throughout the Burma campaign, the great weight of responsibility had fallen on the Indian Army and some 17,000 Indians lost their lives between 1941 and 1945 in the longest single British and Commonwealth land campaign of the war.

OPPOSITE: British Commonwealth soldiers look at a line of Japanese dead after an unsuccessful Japanese counter-attack during the operations around the key town of Meiktila in March 1945. Japanese soldiers continued to fight to the end. For every Allied soldier killed in the reconquest of Burma, there were eight Japanese dead.

ABOVE: Men of the 2nd York and Lancaster Regiment search the ruins of a railway station for Japanese snipers during the advance of the 14th Army to Rangoon along the railway corridor, 13 April 1945.

1 APRIL 1945–2 MAY 1945

VICTORY IN ITALY

As a result of the winter weather and the diversion of resources to other fronts, the campaign in Italy did not begin again until spring 1945.

Allied forces amounted to 17 well-resourced divisions (British, American, Polish, Brazilian, South African, Indian and the New Zealand Division) and substantial airpower. Kesselring, who was replaced in March by Colonel General von Vietinghoff, had 23 divisions, most very under-strength, with an average of 1,700 soldiers in each, little air power and the assistance of two Italian divisions of Marshal Graziani's Army of Liguria, all that was left of the Fascist armed forces.

Alexander planned a major campaign to complete the destruction of Axis forces. Operation "Grapeshot" aimed to encircle the German 14th and 10th armies south of the River Po, almost all of whose bridges had been destroyed long before by Allied air power. The US Fifth Army would attack west of Bologna and then swing eastwards, while the British 8th Army under Lieutenant General McCreery was to force the Argenta Gap on the coast and then swing westwards. After a number of small preliminary operations to tidy up the Allied line, the operation was launched on 9 April when waves of heavy bombers, followed by 200 medium bombers and 500 fighter-bombers, attacked the German line. Already dispirited, and with German commanders trying to negotiate a secret armistice, the German army crumbled quickly and by 17 April Argenta was captured and the way opened to exploit westwards and north towards Venice.

The US Fifth Army opened its part of the offensive on 14 April, moving quickly through the mountains and reaching the outskirts of Bologna by 20 April. Hitler refused von Vietinghoff's request to withdraw and growing numbers of German prisoners were taken as Bologna was encircled by the two Allied armies, who met on 25 April at Finale nell'Emilia. The Po valley provided a much easier battlefield and with little serious opposition remaining the US Fifth Army reached Verona on 26 April, swinging west to take Milan. The 8th Army moved rapidly north, crossing the Po unopposed on 24 April, liberating Venice on 29 April and reaching Trieste on 2 May, just after the arrival of Tito's forces. A German delegation arrived at

Alexander's headquarters at Caserta on 28 April and an armistice was agreed the next day to come into effect on 2 May.

On 28 April Mussolini, still nominal head of the Italian Social Republic, and his mistress Clara Petacci were caught by partisans of the Garibaldi Brigade at Dongo at the head of Lake Como as they made an unsuccessful bid to escape to Switzerland. Mussolini, Clara and other Fascist leaders were executed, their bodies taken to Milan and hung upside down in Piazzale Loreto, where Italian partisans had been murdered some time before. All over northern Italy, cities were liberated by partisan groups even before the arrival of Allied forces. In Milan, on 26 April, the local partisans established their own government before the Americans arrived. What followed was a period of great confusion as the pro-Allied Italian government in Rome tried to co-operate with partisan groups, many of whom were Communists distrustful of other Italian political groups. A coalition was formed in June 1945 under the democrat and anti-Fascist Feruccio Parri which brought together all the groups involved in the struggle to liberate Italy from German rule.

The cost of the long campaign in Italy was very high. The US Fifth Army suffered 188,746 casualties, the 8th Army 123,993. German casualties amounted to at least 435,000. Around 60,000 Italians were killed by bombing attacks, most of them in the last year of the war. The war and the bombing destroyed important parts of Italy's cultural heritage while the divisions between Fascists and partisans left a long residue of bitterness and hostility in Italian society and politics.

OPPOSITE: British 8th Army Royal Artillery troops on 28 April 1945 complete work on a searchlight to illuminate the first pontoon Bailey bridge built across the River Po so that traffic across it can be continuous. Once across the river, Allied armies rapidly occupied the rest of northern Italy.

ABOVE: Sherman tanks and army vehicles in the Piazzale Roma in Venice on 30 April 1945 following the liberation of the city by the British 8th Army the previous day. On 29 April the German army had agreed an armistice.

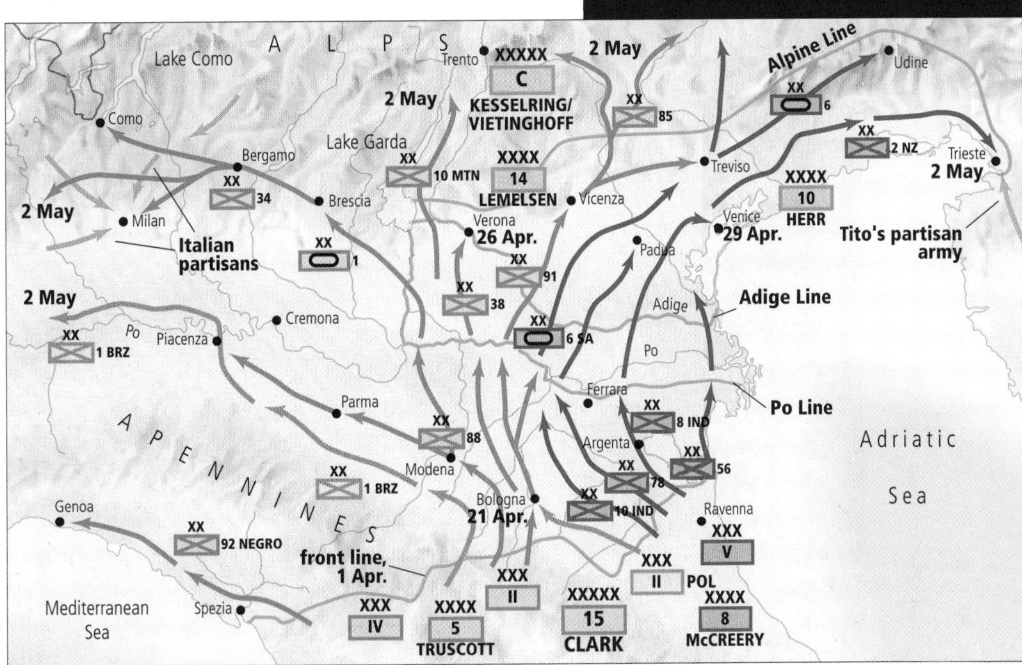

7 MAY–2 SEPTEMBER 1945

SURRENDER IN GERMANY AND JAPAN

The final surrender of remaining Axis forces in Europe was an uncoordinated and messy process.

Though victory in Europe was proclaimed on 8 May, resistance still continued in some parts, while the Soviet Union announced victory on 9 May and declared 11 May as a day of celebration. Even the formal signing of a surrender document had to be done twice to satisfy Soviet sensibilities.

The first surrender came in Italy where a ceasefire, negotiated by General Heinrich von Vietinghoff on 29 April, came into effect on 2 May, the same day as the surrender in Berlin. Some 490,000 German and Axis soldiers were taken prisoner. The surrender of forces in Germany and Austria took place as each area was encircled or captured. On 4 May, German forces in northern Germany and the Netherlands surrendered to Field Marshal Montgomery's 21st Army Group; on 5 May German forces in Bavaria surrendered. Also on

OPPOSITE: Thousands of jubilant Britons crowd into London's Piccadilly Circus on VE Day, 8 May 1945. At 3.00 p.m. Churchill broadcast to the nation from 10 Downing Street ending with the words "Advance Britannia!". His speech was relayed by loudspeakers across central London.

RIGHT: General Alfred Jodl, chief of operations at the German Supreme Command during the war, signs the instrument of unconditional surrender at a schoolhouse in the French city of Rheims, 7 May 1945.

BELOW: Thousands of German soldiers wait to be transported to POW camps after crossing a ruined bridge over the Elbe to surrender to the Western Allies and avoid Soviet captivity, May 1945.

5 May, the new German government in Flensburg ordered Hitler's wartime chief of operations, General Alfred Jodl, to proceed to the French city of Rheims to surrender to the Western Allies, still hoping perhaps that a division could be opened up between the West and Stalin. Eisenhower insisted on unconditional German surrender, as had been the case in all the subsidiary theatres. At 2.40 in the early morning of 7 May, a brief ceremony took place in a schoolhouse in Rheims, which Eisenhower had made his temporary headquarters. Surrounded by Allied officers and 17 invited newsmen, Jodl signed the act of surrender. The Soviet representative, General Susloparov, caught unawares by the capitulation and uncertain about what his instructions from Moscow would be, signed in a way that suggested the possibility of a second ceremony. A little later a directive from Stalin arrived ordering him to sign nothing.

Stalin deeply distrusted his Allies for agreeing to a full German surrender without proper Soviet participation. At a meeting in the Kremlin that night he accused the West of organizing a "shady deal" with the defeated Germans. He refused to accept the Rheims document and pressed his allies to agree to a formal, public ceremony in Berlin, the heart of the enemy war effort. His allies agreed and a second surrender document was prepared in Moscow, which had to be reconciled during the course of 8 May with the Western version. A power failure left the typists completing the draft by candlelight.

Exactly at the stroke of midnight, Field Marshal Keitel led the German delegation into the room in the former German military engineering school. He signed for the Germans, Marshal Zhukov for the Soviet Union, Air Chief Marshal Arthur Tedder for the British Empire, General Carl Spaatz for the Americans and General de Lattre de Tassigny for the French.

By this time the British and American people had already been told about the surrender and 8 May was designated Victory in Europe (VE) Day and a public holiday. Scenes of jubilation, widely photographed in London, were more modest in other parts of the country. During the course of the day, Churchill appeared next to the royal family on the balcony at Buckingham Palace to an ecstatic welcome. The Soviet population were only told about the surrender early in the morning of 9 May, and only two days later was there a formal day of celebration. In central Europe Soviet forces were still fighting against the remnants of Field Marshal Schörner's Army Group Centre which had retreated for a last stand in Czechoslovakia. It was overwhelmed by Konev's 1st Ukrainian Army Group and Malinovsky's 2nd Ukrainian Army Group and finally surrendered on 11–12 May 1945. Elsewhere, news of the surrender was brought to German garrisons in Lorient and St Nazaire on the French Atlantic coast, in the Channel Islands and at the port of Dunkirk, which had all been bypassed in earlier campaigns and never freed. Local documents of surrender had to be signed in Denmark and Norway. It had taken almost a week from Jodl's original instructions for the cumbersome process of unconditional surrender to be completed.

The Allied demand for the unconditional surrender of Japan presented a more difficult process than was the case in Europe. Surrender was deeply dishonourable for the Japanese military, which was why so many Japanese soldiers and sailors fought literally until the last, or committed suicide. The military domination of decision-making in Japan and the prevailing ethos of sacrifice for the sake of the Emperor impeded any attempt by civilian leaders during 1945, faced with the inevitability of defeat, to find a formula that would satisfy both the Allies and the Japanese military.

The Japanese leadership also shared many illusions about the invincibility of Japan and the defensibility of the Empire. Only with the heavy destruction of Japanese cities in 1945 and the bombardment of the homeland by Allied ships and carrier aircraft was it evident to the wider population that the propaganda of victory had been a cruel deception. Yet in the face of defeat the military decided that the Japanese homeland would be defended at all costs under the slogan "The Glorious Death of One Hundred Million". In January 1945, a Homeland Operations Plan was formulated and in March a law passed to enforce the creation of People's Volunteer Units, followed in June by the creation of People's Volunteer Combat Corps. These people's militia were poorly armed and supplied, but the assumption among Japan's military was that death must always be preferable to dishonour.

In April 1945, a new prime minister, Admiral Kantoro Suzuki, was installed. While some efforts were made to see if there was an acceptable formula for an end to hostilities, Suzuki continued to work with military plans for a final defence. On 26 July, the Allies announced the Potsdam Declaration which re-affirmed the demand for unconditional surrender and committed the Allies to the democratic reconstruction of Japan. The stumbling block remained the question of the Emperor: unless the Allies would guarantee the survival of the monarchy, the government would not be able to endorse surrender. Hirohito had already let it be known

LEFT: The Japanese General Yoshijiro Umezu signs the instrument of unconditional surrender on behalf of the Japanese army aboard the battleship USS *Missouri* on 2 September 1945.

OPPOSITE TOP: Troops of the 25th Indian Division searching Japanese POWs in the Malayan capital Kuala Lumpur after they had been disarmed in September 1945.

OPPOSITE BOTTOM: Jubilant Manchurians greet the Soviet army as it enters Port Arthur on 22 August 1945 after a lightning victory over the occupying Japanese Kwantung Army. The Manchurian territory was ceded to China in 1946 and became part of the new Communist People's Republic in 1949.

through the Japanese ambassador in Moscow (Japan and the Soviet Union were not yet at war) that Japan wished to end the war, but his own position made it difficult to deliver what the Allies wanted.

The changed circumstances of early August forced the hand of the Japanese government. On 6 August, the first atomic bomb was dropped and on 8–9 August, before the bomb on Nagasaki, Soviet forces opened up a major offensive against the Japanese Kwantung Army in Manchuria. The Soviet army expected a hard fight in difficult terrain, but so weakened was Japanese capability that the million men, 5,000 tanks and 5,000 aircraft of the Far Eastern army groups overwhelmed Japanese opposition within six days, with the deaths of 80,000 Japanese. On 9 August, Suzuki finally asked the Emperor to decide on surrender or a final fight to the death and the Emperor, who had already had secret intimations from the Americans that the throne would be protected, opted for surrender. He had to repeat his decision at an imperial conference on 14 August, and the following day, despite continued opposition from the military, he made an unprecedented broadcast to his people that Japan would surrender.

The final process proved as messy as it had been in Europe. Some Japanese soldiers continued to fight on weeks after the decision to surrender. Many could not be reached in distant outposts and garrisons and the Allied troops had great difficulty in persuading them that the surrender was actually true. In Manchuria, formal surrender came only on 21 August and fighting continued in some areas until September. On 2 September, aboard the battleship USS *Missouri* in Tokyo Bay, Japanese representatives met with General MacArthur to sign the formal instruments of surrender. Japanese forces surrendered in China on 9 September, in Burma on 13 September and in Hong Kong on 16 September. Japan was occupied by American and British Commonwealth forces; the Emperor was not deposed and played an important part in the democratic reconstruction of his country.

INDEX

PICTURE CREDITS

The vast majority of photographs reproduced in this book have been taken from the collections of the photograph archive at the Imperial War Museum. The museum's reference numbers for each photograph is indicated below, giving the page on which they appear and location indicator.

Key: t = top, b = bottom, l = left, r = right and c = centre

Imperial War Museum: 1, 127bl (B 5071), 6b (MED 914), 11tr (D 2597), 12 (A2), 13tr (UNI 12861), 15t (HU 55640), 16 (HU 28737) 16t (N 229), 17 (H 15384), 19t (F 2036), 20 (NYP 68075), 21tr (IWM (HU 2286) 21tl (HU 1135), 22b (H 2280), 23t (F 4849), 23b (H 1647), 24 (HU 2283), 26t (HU 3266), 27b (D 1966), 28 (CH 740), 29 (CH 1398), 30t (CH 1827), 30b (CH 1401), 33 (ME_RAF 892), 34 (H 3233), 35t (H 3096), 35b (A 10296), 36 (HU 44272), 37 (HU 1129), 38 (H 5593) 39b (D 5984), 41r (CM 164), 41l (A 9760), 42t (A 3532), 43b (A 20659), 44 (CM 354), 45br (E 1766), 47b (E 3265_E), 48t (E 3020_E), 49t (MH 6100), 49b (HU 1997), 49c (MH 6100), 47t (E 3282), 50 (A 4217), 51b (A 4100), 51t (A 4386), 52 (E 2887), 53t (HU 5625), 54 (E4087), 55t (CM 774), 57 (E 6577), 58b (E 6839), 58t (E 9569), 61bl (HU 2779), 63 (HU 2770), 64 (D 8896), 65t (N 459), 66t (F 492), 66b (N 481), 66c (H 17365), 69t (A 8701), 68 (A 11155), 69b (CM 3697), 73b (SE 3310), 74 (TR 11), 80 (A 11231), 83b (INS 8038), 84t (TR 1776), 85tl (E 8487), 85tr (E 15223), 85b (TR 2283), 86 (E 18474), 87tr (INS 5132), 87tl (INS 5110), 88b (E 18980), 89tr (E 21333), 89b (E 18971), 92 (SE 7910), 93 (MH 7877), 94br (INS 7092), 94tr (HU 6643), 95 (SE 7921), 96l (SE 7946), 96r, 97 (IND 2290), 99 (NA 2876), 100 (C 3717), 102t (HU 92132), 102b (CH 18005), 103b (CH 11047), 104l (FLM 2239/40/42), 104-105 (HU 4594), 106 (A 17916), 107t (INS 5154), 108 (NA 6330), 109tr (A 19246), 109tl (NA 6157), 112 (A 20687), 113b (A 22633), 113t (A 21200), 114 (NA 11041), 115tr (INS 5463), 115tl (NA 12136), 115b (NA 15306), 116t (MH 11250), 117t (MH 1978), 120 (IND 3479), 122b (IND 3430), 123tl (INS 4079), 123b (IND 3331), 124 (B 5103), 125t (B5091), 127t (TR 2626), 127br (B 5114), 128 (B 8441), 129 (FLA 5499), 130t (B 6781), 130b (B 7649), 132 (CL 3430), 133tl(C 4431), 133bl (D 21213), 135 CL 1725), 136 (TR 2287), 138 (HU 21013), 139 (V 170), 141b (H 6293), 141t (HU 20288), 142 (CL 1173), 144tr (TR 174), 144l (B 10124_A), 144r (HU 2126), 145t (HU 2129), 145b (BU 1121), 146 (B 14413), 147 (BU 2636), 149 (BU 4269), 150 (IND 4592), 151tl (SE 3773), 151b (SE 3804), 151tr (IND 3143), 152 (TR 2846), 153 (NA 24683), 154 (EA 65879), 155t (EA 65715), 156 (A 20427_A), 157t (IND 4848)

The publishers would also like to thank the following sources for their kind permission to reproduce the photographs in this book.

AKG-Images: 6t, 25, 53b, 77t, 101, 122t, 134, /Ullstein Bild: 62b, 81t, 157b, 103t,

Corbis: /Auschitz Museum: 148; /Bettmann: 15b, 18, 32, 43t, 56, 61br, 70, 110, 123tr; /Hulton-Deutsch Collection: 7b, 14, 73t,

Getty Images: 9, 10t, 10b, 16b, 39t, 59b, 62t/AFP: 8; /Popperfoto: 140; /Time & Life Pictures: 4, 5tr, 71, 72, 82, 94bl, 155b

Mary Evans Picture Library: 84b

National Archives and Records Administration, Washington: 78, 79b, 79t,

Photo12.com: 42b

Press Association Images: AP Photo/Eddie Worth: 3; /DPA: 75

Scala Archives: 119

Topfoto.co.uk: 13tl, 40, 67b, 67t, 89tl, 118; /Ullstein Bild: 59t, 61t, 88t, 98, 133tr

All other items photographed by Karl Adamson

Every effort has been made to acknowledge correctly and contact the source and/or copyright holder of each picture and Carlton Books Limited apologises for any unintentional errors or omissions, which will be corrected in future editions of this book.

MEMORABILIA ON THE PAGE
Imperial War Museum: pages 7t, 9t, 22t, 31, 90, 91, 131
The National Archives of the United States of America: pages 111
The National Archives, Kew: page 126